U0115716

"中国民间武术经典"丛书
Chinese Folk Wushu Classic Series

陈氏太极拳十九势

THE NINETEEN POSTURES OF CHEN-STYLE TAIJI QUAN

丛书主编　陈自强
Chief Editor　Chen Ziqiang

编　著　陈自强
Compiler　Chen Ziqiang

翻　译　郭　勇　王青云　胡大鹏　约瑟夫·戴维(英国)
Translators　Guo Yong　Wang Qingyun　Hu Dapeng　Joseph Davey(Great Britain)

海燕出版社
PETREL PUBLISHING HOUSE

河南电子音像出版社
HENAN ELECTRONIC & AUDIOVISUAL PRESS

图书在版编目(CIP)数据

陈氏太极拳十九势：汉英对照 / 陈自强著；郭勇等译. — 郑州：海燕出版社，2008.8
（中国民间武术经典）
ISBN 978-7-5350-3793-0

Ⅰ.陈…　Ⅱ.①陈…②郭…　Ⅲ.太极拳—套路（武术）—中国—汉、英　Ⅳ.G852.11

中国版本图书馆CIP数据核字（2008）第077902号

陈氏太极拳十九势
THE NINETEEN POSTURES OF CHEN-STYLE TAIJI QUAN

出版发行：海燕出版社　河南电子音像出版社
Publish: Petrel Publishing House　Henan Electronic & Audiovisual Press
地址：河南省郑州市经五路66号
Add: No.66 Jingwu Road, Zhengzhou, Henan Province, China
邮编：450002
Pc: 450002
电话：+86-371-65720922
Tel: +86-371-65720922
传真：+86-371-65731756
Fax: +86-371-65731756

印刷：郑州龙洋印务有限公司
开本：850×1168　1/16
印张：8.25
字数：107千字
印数：1000—2000册
版次：2008年8月郑州第1版
印次：2015年6月第2次印刷
书号：ISBN 978-7-5350-3793-0
定价：35.00元

前 言
Foreword

中华武术源远流长，各门各派均有其精华之奥妙，同是中华民族的宝贵遗产。而太极拳是我国武术百花园中的一枝奇葩，并逐渐普及到世界的每一个地方，深受人们的喜爱。

陈家沟陈氏第九世祖陈王廷，在祖传拳械基础上依据传统阴阳辩证哲理，结合中医经络学、导引吐纳术，又采众家之所长，创编出一套具有刚柔互济、快慢相间、缠丝连绵、松活弹抖、风格独特、深具民族文化底蕴、符合人体生理与自然运转规律一系列的拳法。其拳理阴阳、理根太极，故名：太极拳。

陈氏太极拳是各派太极拳的始源，从陈家沟陈氏第九世祖陈王廷创编太极拳以来，几百年世代沿袭，历久不衰，并不断发展，又相继演变出杨、吴、武、孙各派的太极拳。

为了世人更好地了解陈氏太极拳，为了能对初学者起到引导作用，同时也为了适应教学，在听取父辈和广大学员的意见和要求的基础上，总结了教学经验。希望广大太极拳爱好者提出宝贵意见，以便今后修改订正。

Chinese Wushu has a long history and the marvelous essence of various schools has been priceless legacy of Chinese people. As a wonderful work of Chinese Wushu, Taijiquan is spreading throughout the world and winning much popularity.

Chen Wangting, the 9th generation ancestor of Chen family in Chenjiagou, according to the traditional negative (*Yin*) and positive (*Yang*) dialectical philosophy, meridian knowledge of traditional Chinese medicine, Taoist breathing exercise method and learning from various schools, created a series of boxing techniques and weapons on the basis of ancestral boxing and weapons. It is unique in style, rich in national cultural elements and is abiding by body physiological and nature operating law which is featured by coupling hardness with slow movement continuous silk reeling energy and action with relaxation and flexibility. Its boxing theory comes from the negative (*Yin*) and the positive (*Yang*) and the root of the theory comes from Supreme Ultimate (Taiji), hence its name Taijiquan.

Chen Family Taijiquan is the origin of Taijiquan of various schools and since the creation of Taijiquan by the 9th generation, Chen Wangting, it has been carried on for several centuries. During the course of its development, it evolved into Taijiquan schools of Yang style, Wú style, Wǔ style and Sun style.

This book aims to make people know more about Chen Family Taijiquan and serves as guidelines for beginners. Meanwhile, in order to make it suitable for teaching, opinions and requirements from people of father's generation and learners have been collected. We hope that Taijiquan enthusiasts can provide suggestions for future revision.

陈自强

Chen Ziqiang

2008年6月

June 2008

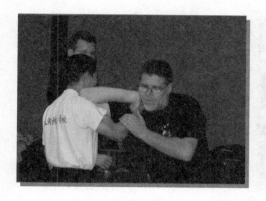

作者陈自强（中）在德国教授警察局局长练习陈氏太极推手。
The author Chen Ziqiang (the center) is teaching pushing-hands in Germany to the head of police.

陈家沟太极拳学校校长陈小星大师（左一）在美国教授拳术。
The headmaster of Chenjiagou Taijiquan School Chen Xiaoxing (the first from the left) visits America to teach Taijiquan.

陈家沟陈氏太极拳第十九世掌门人陈小旺大师（右一），在美国传授太极拳"四两拨千斤"功夫时的情景。
The 19th generation grandmaster of Chen-style Taijiquan, Chen Xiaowang (the first from the right) teaches Taiji in America.

2000年，作者陈自强（左）参加河南省举办的太极拳锦标赛。

In the year of 2000, the author Chen Ziqiang (the left) took part in the Henan Provincal Taijiquan Championship and were photographed together.

2003年，陈家沟陈氏第十九世掌门人陈小旺大师，率领30多个国家的代表回访学校，交流切磋合影留念。

In 2003, the 19th generation grandmaster Chen Xiaowang brought the representatives from over of 30 countries to Chenjiagou Taijiquan School for discussion and cultural exchange.

全国政协副主席陈奎元在视察陈家沟太极拳学校时与部分师生合影留念。

Vice chairman of the Chinese Peoples' Political Consultative Conference, Chen Kuiyuan, is photographed with students while visiting Chenjiagou Taijiquan School.

陈家沟太极拳学校参加在八达岭举办的"同一个世界同一个梦想"的揭牌仪式。

Chenjiagou Taijiquan School joins the opening ceremony of celebrating "One world, One dream" on the starting point of the Great Wall.

在纪念陈氏太极拳祖师爷陈王廷诞辰400周年年会上，作者陈自强（前排中）带领学员为来宾表演陈氏太极拳。

Under direction of the author Master Chen Ziqiang (front center), the students of Chenjiagou celebrate the Chen Wangting's 400th birthday with a special performance.

陈小星校长为学生做动作示范。

The headmaster Chen Xiaoxing demonstrating forms for students.

作者陈自强（前排左一）带领外国学员在中央电视台"乡村大世界"栏目表演陈氏太极拳。

The author Chen Ziqiang (front, the first from the left) leads foreign students in a Taiji performance for "Country World" broadcasted by CCTV.

作者陈自强（中）在陕西佛教圣地法门寺传授陈氏太极拳。

The author Chen Ziqiang (the center) teaching Taijiquan in the Buddhist Famen temple in Sha'anxi Province.

作者陈自强（左五）在德国汉堡教授太极拳时与学员合影。

The author Chen Ziqiang (the fifth from the left) with students in Hamburg, Germany while teaching Taijiquan.

作者陈自强（左五）在西班牙教授陈氏太极拳时与学员合影。

The author Chen Ziqiang (the fifth from the left) with students in Spain while teaching Chen-style Taijiquan.

陈家沟太极拳学校校长陈小星（左四），偕学校部分师生与美国著名摇滚歌星Lou Reed（左五）合影，左一为作者。

The headmaster of Chenjiagou Taijiquan School Chen Xiaoxing (the fourth from the left) along with students of the school were photographed with Rock and Roll legend Lou Reed (the fifth from the left). The author is standing among them (the first from the left).

在马鞍山国际太极拳交流大赛中，陈家沟太极拳学校获奖学员合影。

The students from Chenjiagou Taijiquan School were award the winners in the Ma'anshan International Taijiquan conference.

"中国民间武术经典" 丛书

Chinese Folk Wushu Classic Series

编写委员会 **Editorial Board**

主 任　Director

高明星 （河南电子音像出版社社长、编审）

Gao Mingxing, Proprietor and Copy Editor of Henan Electronic &

Audiovisual Press

副主任　Assistant Director

陈自强 （陈家沟陈氏太极拳学校副校长兼总教练）

Chen Ziqiang, Vice President and General Coach of Chenjiagou Taijiquan School

Education Office

杨东军 （河南电子音像出版社总编辑、编审）

Yang Dongjun, Chief Editor and Copy Editor of Henan Electronic &

Audiovisual Press

段嫩芝 （河南电子音像出版社编审）

Duan Nenzhi, Copy Editor of Henan Electronic & Audiovisual Press

李 惠 （河南省体育局武术运动管理中心副主任）

Li Hui, Assistant Director of Wushu Center of Henan Province Physical

总策划　Chief Producer

高明星 Gao Mingxing

责任编辑　Editors in Charge

刘聪玲　　连孝善

Liu Congling　Lian Xiaoshan

"中国民间武术经典"丛书
Chinese Folk Wushu Classic Series

作者名单 Author List

主 编　Chief Editor

陈自强　Chen Ziqiang

编 委　Members of the Editorial Board

崔武装	陈 炳	郑广济	崔恒全	陈 恩
Cui Wuzhuang	Chen Bing	Zheng Guangji	Cui Hengquan	Chen En

任广义	单 伟	朱建军	曾卓儿
Ren Guangyi	Shan Wei	Zhu Jianjun	Zeng Zhuoer

视频示范　Video Performers

陈自强	陈自军	陈 辉	岳建勇
Chen Ziqiang	Chen Zijun	Chen Hui	Yue Jianyong

阎子腾	赵艳芳
Yan Ziteng	Zhao Yanfang

动作示范　Illustrator

陈自强　Chen Ziqiang

摄 影　Photographer

林伟峰　Lin Weifeng

目 录

Chapter I Overview

OVERVIEW

第一章 陈氏太极拳概述

第一节
陈氏太极拳渊源、发展及演变
THE ORIGIN, DEVELOPMENT AND
EVOLUTION OF CHEN-STYLE TAIJIQUAN

太极拳是中华民族武术宝库中一颗璀璨的明珠，它以其高超的技击性、绝妙的健身性和精美的艺术性，越来越受到世界各国人民的青睐。而具有阴阳转换、刚柔互济的太极拳究竟起源于哪里，这是很多人所关注的问题。

研究武术的名家唐豪同志，曾于1930至1932年间，三下陈家沟调查考证太极拳的起源，历时数月之久。其间，唐豪同志查阅了《中州文献辑》、《温县县志》及《三三六》拳谱，并拍摄了陈氏太极拳历代人物的遗像、遗物、碑文，以及陈家沟世代流传至今的陈氏太极拳拳照。经考察多方面历史资料证实，太极拳的创始人就是明末清初河南省温县陈家沟陈氏第九世祖陈王廷。

陈家沟陈氏始祖陈卜，原籍山西泽州郡（今山西晋城），明朝洪武五年（1372年）迁至河南沁阳县（今温县武德镇）。因陈氏始祖为人忠厚，谦诚待人，德高望重，深受乡里拥戴，故将其居住地命名为陈卜庄，沿用至今。后因地势低洼，不宜居住，搬到了位于温县城东青风岭上的常阳村。随着陈氏人丁兴旺，常阳村遂改名为陈家沟。

始祖精通拳械，历世相传直至清乾隆十九年（1754年），始立《陈氏家谱》，距迁来之时已逾三百年。其间人物事迹缺乏文字记载，有关拳术也无著述。第九世祖陈王廷晚年开始隐居造拳，但其有关著作因年代久远多遭遗失，现仅存《拳经总歌》和《长短句》辞一首。辞中说："蒙恩赐，枉徒然，到而今年老残喘，只落得《黄庭》一卷随身伴。闷来时造拳，忙来时耕田，趁余闲，教下些弟子儿孙，成龙成虎任方便……"由此可见，因当时社会动荡，时途不顺，其不得志才隐居造拳，以解毕生之志向。

陈王廷文武兼备，依据祖传拳械，博采诸家拳法之精华，结合中医经络学和导引吐纳术，以中华传统阴阳学说为理论依据，创编了武术、传统文化、医学三者相融合的流传至今的"陈氏太极拳"。

Due to its delicate sense of artistry and awesome body building methods, Taijiquan is a resplendent treasure of Chinese Wushu to which more and more people have began to pay attention. With its unique exchange of *Yin* and *Yang*, firmness and gentleness, the question of Taiji's origin is one that many might ask.

A wushu research celebrity Mr Tang Hao, during the period of 1930 to 1932, visited the Chenjiagou Village three times doing research into the origins of Taijiquan, which lasted for several months. Tang Hao consulted various historical materials such as *Documents of Central China*, *Records of Wen County's Historical Events* as well as *The Old Footage of Chen-style Taiji*. His research showed clear historical evidence that Taijiquan was created towards the end of Ming dynasty and the beginning of the Qing dynasty in the Chenjiagou Village, Wen County, Henan.

The ninth generation of the Chen family, Chen Wangting was the descendant of Chen Bu who was born in Zezhou County, the present Jin County of Shanxi Province during the fifth year of the Ming dynasty in 1372. He then moved to Qinyang County, Henan Province, known today as Wude Town, Wen County. The ancestors of the Chen family had a reputation as being sincere and kind to people, who became highly respected among the people of the town, thus its name was changed to Chen Bu Village, a name still in use to this day. Later, due to the low terrain being unsuitable for family living they moved again to Changyang Village of Dong Qingfengling, to the east of Wen County. As the popularity of the Chen family grew the name of Changyang Village was changed to the Chenjiagou Village.

The ancestors that mastered the quan forms transmitted them down through generations until Emperor Qianlong era in Qing dynasty in 1754 wrote the *Chen Family Tree*. This was over 300 years ago and the records of people and events are lacking, as is the earliest records of the quan forms, allegedly hidden by the ninth generation master, Chen Wangting. Though his books are lost due to the passage of time there are still *Songs of Quan* and *Long and Short Phase* left. One song says, "Honored by gifts from heaven, wasted untill old age. Now at this old age, I have nothing left but the *Book of Huangting* (the foremost important Taoist classic). Creating boxing when I am idle, cropping in the fields when I am busy, other times, I teach my children and students, so that they would become dragons or tigers as they wish..."

Chen Wangting, living in seclusion to create the quan, was learned in both cultural pursuits and Wushu. In keeping with the essence of his own family quan, he incorporated various other quan styles as well as combining an awareness of the energy channels of Chinese medical theory with Chinese traditional *Yin* and *Yang* theory. Thus today's modern Chen-style Taijiquan is born out of a combination of wushu, medical theory and Chinese traditional culture.

第二节
陈氏太极拳歌诀
FORMULAS OF CHEN-STYLE TAIJIQUAN

一、长短句
Long and Short Phrase

　　叹当年，披坚执锐，扫荡群氛，几次颠险。蒙恩赐，枉徒然，到而今年老残喘，只落得《黄庭》一卷随身伴。闷来时造拳，忙来时耕田，趁余闲，教下些弟子儿孙，成龙成虎任方便。欠官粮早完，要私债即还，骄谄勿用，忍让为先。人人道我憨，人人道我颠，常洗耳不弹。冠咲杀那万户诸侯兢兢业业，不如俺心中常舒泰。名利总不贪，参透机关，识破邯郸，陶情于渔水盘桓乎山川。兴也无干，废也无干。若得个世景安泰，恬淡如常，不忮不求，听其自然。那管他世态炎凉，权衡相参。成也无关，败也无关，谁是神仙？我是神仙！

In amour with my sword, I fought courageously in the competitive society, survived several great dangers in the blessing from the imperial, all means nothing. Now at this old age, I have nothing left but the Book of Huangting (the foremost important Taoist classic). Creating boxing when I am idle, cropping in the fields when I am busy, other times, I teach my children and students, so that they would become dragons or tigers as they wish. Paying off taxes and debts, am I humble and excising forbearance? I am told foolish and crazy, I listen reverently, but I pursue no officialdoms so I sneer at the Marquises. Awaken in the wisdom, I roam in the waters and the mountains. Victory or fall matters naught. In peace as I am always, nothing to go for but live freely. Who care about the hostility and consultation? Success is so, failure is so. Who is the immortal? Am I not one?

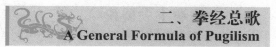

纵放屈伸人莫知，诸靠缠绕我皆依。

劈打推压得进步，搬撂横采也难敌。

钩掤逼揽人人晓，闪惊巧取有谁知。

佯输诈走谁云败，引诱回冲致胜归。

滚拴搭扫灵微妙，横直劈砍奇更奇。

截进遮拦穿心肘，迎风接步红炮捶。

二换扫压挂面脚，左右边簪桩跟脚。

截前压后无缝锁，防东击西要熟识。

上拢下提君须记，进攻退闪莫迟迟。

藏头盖面天下有，攒心剁胁世间稀。

老师不识此中理，难将武艺论高低。

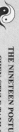

Opponents do not know what footwork and handwork will be used by me, I will depend on push-hands and silk reeling energy.

Split, hit, push and press must go with footwork, hard to know the next step to attack or to defend.

Everyone knows the handworks, but who can make use of it fast and skillfully.

Early to say one is loser when he pretends to lose and retreat, right to win after returning to attack.

Wonderful it is to seize up and down, even amazing to hit from all around.

Intercept and advance by heart-directed elbow, in case of failure cannon fist can be used.

Twice change of hand to rise, two hands separate to crotch attack.

No risks are provided for any handwork, bear in mind of protecting east and attacking west.

Up empty and down lifted is to be remembered, advance and retreat is not to be delayed.

Covering head and face to defend is everywhere, attacking the vital part to defend is almost nowhere.

Theories here are not understood by the master, martial skills are hard to be commented as high or low.

1. 理 Law (Li)

夫物散必有统，分必有合，天地间四面八方，纷纷者各有所属，千头万绪，攘攘者自有其源。盖一本可散为万殊，而万殊咸归于一本，拳术之学亦不外此公例。夫太极拳者，千变万化，无往非劲，势虽不侔，而劲归于一；夫所谓一者，自顶至足，内有脏腑筋骨，外有肌肤皮肉，四肢百骸相联而为一者也。破之而不开，撞之而不散，上欲动而下自随之，下欲动而上自领之，上下动而中部应之，中部动而上下和之，内外相连，前后相需，所谓一以贯之者，其斯之谓欤！而要非勉强以致之，袭焉而为之也。当时而动，如龙如虎，出乎尔而，急如电闪。当时而静，寂然湛然，居其所而稳如山岳。且静无不静，表里上下全无参差牵挂之意，动无不动，前后左右均无游疑抽扯之形，洵乎若水之就下，沛然莫能御之也。若火机之内攻，发之而不及掩耳。不暇思索，不烦拟议，诚不期然而已然。盖劲以积日而有益，功以久练而后成。观圣门一贯之学，必俟多闻强识格物致知方能有功；是知事无难易，功惟自进，不可躐等，不可急就，按步就序，循序渐进，夫而后百骸筋节，自相贯通，上下表里不难联络，庶乎散者统之，分者合之，四肢百骸总归于一气矣。

For all the matters in the universe the scattered will be led, the divided will be reunited, each one has its owner and all can find their sources. Therefore the same matter can scatter in different forms while the different forms can be grouped into one kind, which can be applied to Taijiquan techniques. Taijiquan full of changes, move with energy which despite different positions is threaded together as one. One here means the connection of all the limbs and bones form head to feet including viscera and physique inside and skin and muscles outside. It cannot be broken up or divided by strike. When the upper part tends to move, the lower will follow naturally. When the lower tends to move, the upper will lead naturally. When the upper and lower parts move, the middle complies, and when the middle moves, the upper and lower parts coordinate so that all are linked as a whole. It is not formed by intentional efforts but the state in case of attack. If one moves, he shall move powerfully as a dragon or tiger and quickly as lightning. If one keeps still, he has deep stillness, looks firm as mountains in his place. Furthermore stillness covers no stillness failures which show no signs of links and difference between the outside and inside, the up and down. Motions covers no motionlessness and there is no signs of wavering for the front and back, the right and left, so it is like the falling water which is hard to defend.

If the chances are right for attack, the speed will be amazingly high with no time to think or consult and the unexpected effects will be reached. As to energy time will help and to go on practice makes perfect while to the wholeness wide knowledge and various investigation are important. It is known that no matter how the things cannot be defined as easy or diff icult. *Gong* depends on one's own efforts for progress which cannot be slowed down or sped up, but follow the steps to advance gradually and then all the bones and muscles, up and down, outside and inside, will be linked naturally and thus the scattered are led and the divided are reunited which means all the limbs and bones become a whole.

2. 气 Breath (Qi)

天地间未有一往而不返者，亦未常有直而无曲者矣；盖物有对待，势有回还，古今不易之理也。常有世之论捶者，而兼论气者矣。夫主于一何分为二？所谓二者即呼吸也，呼吸即阴阳也。捶不能无动静，气不能无呼吸。呼则为阳，吸则为阴；上升为阳，下降为阴；阳气上升而为阳，阳气下行而为阴；阴气上升即为阳，阴气下行仍为阴，此阴阳之所以分也。何谓清浊？升而上者为清，降而下者为浊。清者为阳，浊者为阴，然分而言之为阴阳，浑而言之统为气；气不能无阴阳，即所谓人不能无动静，鼻不能无呼吸，口不能无出入，而所以为对待回还之理也。然则气分为二，而贯于一，有志于是途者，慎勿以是为拘拘焉耳。

In the universe, there is nothing which goes and never returns and nothing which keep straight and never bend, so the truth will never change that there are two opposite sides for everything and there is return of position. When theories about fists come up some also express the opinion about *Qi*. As the owner is one, why it is divided into two parts? Exhalation is positive (*Yang*) and inhalation is negative (*Yin*). The fists inhalation (*Xi*) and exhalation (*Hu*) must have movements and likewise, breath (*Qi*) must have exhalation, the rise of *Qi* (breath) is *Yang* and fall is *Yin*. The rise of *Yang qi* is *Yang* and the fall of it is *Yin* while the rise of *Yin qi* is *Yang* and the fall of it is *Yin*, which is the difference between *Yin* and *Yang*. As to clearness (*Qing*) and unclearness (*Zhuo*), the rising up one is clearness which stands for *Yang* and the falling down one is unclearness which stands for *Yin*. So the dividing parts are named *Yin* and *Yang* while the reunited is named breath. Breath must have *Yin* and *Yang*, just as human must have stillness and movements the nose must have inhalation and exhalation, and mouth must have going out and coming which is law of the opposites and return. Though breath is divided into two parts, it is linked together as one, which shall be understood by the one who is interested in that.

3. 三节 Three Parts (Jie)

夫气本诸身，而身节部甚繁，若逐节论之，则有远乎拳术之宗旨，惟分为三节而论，可谓得其截法；三节上、中、下，或根、中、梢也。以一身言之：头为上节，胸为中节，腿为下节。以头面言之：额为上节，鼻为中节，口为下节。以中身言之：胸为上节，腹为中节，丹田为下节。以腿言之：胯为根节，膝为中节，足为梢节。以臂言之：膊为根节，肘为中节，手为梢节。以手言之：腕为根节，掌为中节，指为梢节。观于此，而足不必论矣。然则自项至足，莫不各有三节也；要之，即莫非三节之所，即莫非着意之处。盖上节不明，无依无宗。中节不明，满腔是空。下节不明，颠覆必生。由此观之，身三节部，岂可忽也。至于气之发动，要从梢节起，中节随，根节催之而已。此固分而言之；若合而言之，则上自头顶，下至足底，四肢百骸，总为一节，夫何为三节之有哉，又何三节中之各有三节云乎哉！

Breath is a matter of one thing while the parts of the body are varied. If they are discussed part by part, it goes far away from the aim of boxing techniques. In truth it can serve the purpose by discussing them by three parts: the upper, the middle and the lower, or root, middle and tip. For the entire body, head is the upper part, chest is the middle part and legs are the lower part. For the face, forehead is the upper, nose is the middle and mouth is the lower. For the middle body, chest is the upper, stomach is the middle and Dantian is the lower. For the legs, hip is root, knee is middle and feet is tip. For the upper limb, arm is root, elbow is middle and hand is tip. For the hand, wrist is root, palm is middle and finger is tip, from which the case of feet can be known. So there are three parts from neck to feet. It is important to focus on the three parts and their cooperation. If the upper is not clear, there will be no source, if the middle is not clear, the internal body will be empty, and if the lower not clear, the overturn will occur. From this, it is obvious that the three parts of the body cannot be overlooked. In terms of the three parts, the development of breath begins from tip is followed by middle and is sped up by the root, while in terms of the entire body, from the top of head to the bottom of feet, all the limbs and bones is one part, there will be no three parts for the body and for each part.

4. 四梢 Four Tips (Shao)

试于论身之外，而进论四梢。夫四梢者，身之余绪也；言身者初不及此，言气者亦所罕闻，然捶以由内而发外，气本诸身而发梢，气之为用，不本诸身，则虚而不实；不行于梢，则实而仍虚；梢亦可弗讲乎！若手指足特论身之梢耳！而未及梢之梢也。四梢惟何，发其一也。夫发之所系，不列于五行，无关于四体，是无足论矣；然发为血之梢，血为气之海，纵不本诸发而论气，要不可离乎血以生气；不离乎血，即不得不兼乎发。发欲冲冠，血梢足矣。抑舌为肉之梢，而肉为气之囊；气不能行诸肉之梢，即气无以充其气之量；故必舌欲催齿，而肉梢足矣。至于骨梢者，齿也；筋梢者，指甲也。气生于骨而联于筋，不及乎齿，即不及乎骨之梢；不及乎指甲，即不及乎筋之梢。而欲足尔者，要非齿欲断筋，甲欲透骨不能也。果能如此，则四梢足矣。四梢足，而气自足矣。岂复有虚而不实，实而仍虚之弊乎！

Besides body, the tips will also be discussed which are what is left of the body. When the body is talked, it is not mentioned at the beginning and it is rarely covered when breath is discussed. However, the fist is developed and produced from the inside to the outside, and breath comes from the body and is produced by the tip. If breath is used without the body it will be insubstantial, and without reaching the tip it seems substantial but in fact insubstantial, so how can the tips be not discussed? If tips refer to finger and foot, it is not the tip of the tips. Then what are the four tips? Hair is one of them. Hair does not belong to the five elements (metal, wood, water, fire and earth) or the four components of the body, which seems worthless to mention, but the hair is the tip of blood, and blood is the sea of breath, so hair shall be included when breath is talked about and bloods cannot be overlooked for producing breath, which means hair shall also be included and tips of blood will be sufficient if hair seems to go out of the hat. Tongue is the tip of muscles which is the bag of breath, so if the breath can go to the tip of muscles, the breath cannot fill its amount and thus tips of muscles will be sufficient if the tongue seems to force the teeth. As to the tip of bones, it is teeth and tip of joints is the fingernail. Breath originates from the bone and is connected by joints. If it does not reach teeth, it does not come to the tip of bones, while if it does not reach the fingernail, it does not come to the tip of joints. If the tips are to be sufficient, teeth seem to break away from the joints and the fingernail seems to go into the bones. If the above state can be met, the four tips are sufficient, which means the breath is sufficient and the situation of the insubstantial and the false substantial can be avoided.

5. 五脏 Five Internal Organs

夫捶以言势，势以言气，人得五脏以成形，即由五脏而生气。五脏实为性命之源，生气之本，而名为心、肝、脾、肺、肾也。心属火，而有炎上之象。肝属木，而有曲直之形。脾属土，而有敦厚之势。肺属金，而有从革之能。肾属水，而有润下之功。此乃五脏之意而犹准之于气，皆有所配合焉。凡世之讲拳术者，要不能离乎斯也。其在于内胸廓为肺经之位，而肺为五脏之华；盖故肺经动，而诸脏不能不动也。两乳之中为心，而肺抱护之。肺之下膈之上，心经之位也。心为君，心火动，而相火无不奉命焉；而两乳之下，右为肝，左为脾，背之十四骨节为肾，至于腰为两肾之本位，而为先天之第一，又为诸脏之根源。故肾足，则金、木、水、火、土无不各显生机焉。此论五脏之部位也。然五脏之存乎内者，各有定位；而见于身者，亦有专属，但地位甚多，难以尽述。大约身之所系，中者属心，窝者属肺，骨之露处属肾，筋之联处属肝，肉之厚处属脾。想其意，心如猛，肝如箭，脾之力大甚无穷，肺经之位最灵变，肾气之动快如风，是在当局者自为体验，而非笔墨所能尽罄者也。

Position is included for the topic of fist which is included for breath which is produced by the five internal organs (viscera)—bases for the figure of human. Five internal organs—heart, liver, spleen, lung and kidney—are the sources of life and places to produce breath. Heart is fire with the appearance of flame, liver is wood with straight and curved forms, spleen is earth with the state of thickness, lung is metal with the leather function and kidney is water with the role of moistening the lower part of the body, all of which are linked with the breath by cooperation and cannot be ignored when the boxing technique is discussed. Lung, at the inside of thoracic cavity, is the essence of the five internal organs, and if the lung moves, other organs will follow. Heart, located between the breasts, protected by the lungs below the lung and above the diaphragm, is the king and the movement of fire from heart will be the command for other organs to follow. Below the breast, the right is liver and the left is spleen, and at the fourteenth backbone is kidney. Waist is the proper position which is born the most important and is the source of all the organs, therefore if the kidney is sufficient, the five elements of metal, wood, water, fire and earth will show the state of vitality. The above is the position of the five internal organs, but as to the location of them on different people, it is difficult to have a detailed description. Generally for the body, the middle belongs to heart, the pit lung, the protrusion of bones kidney, the links of joints liver and the thick muscles spleen. The features of the organs that can be concluded as heart is like fierce animals, liver is like arrow, spleen has limitless strength, the position of lung meridian is the most flexible and the movement of kidney, breath is fast like wind, which can only be understood by one's own experience but not by words here.

6. 三合 Three Cooperation

五脏既明，再论三合。夫所谓三合者，心与意合，气与力合，筋与骨合，内三合也。手与足合，肘与膝合，肩与胯合，外三合也。若以左手与右足相合，左肘与右膝相合，左肩与右胯相合，右三与左亦然。以头与手合，手与身合，身与步合，孰非外合。心与目合，肝与筋合，脾与肉合，肺与身合，肾与骨合，孰非内合。然此特从变而言之也。总之，一动而无不动，一合而无不合，五脏百骸悉在其中矣。

Since the five internal organs are clear, it comes to three cooperation, which means three internal cooperation of heart and *Yi* (consciousness), breath and strength, and muscles and bones and three external cooperation of hand and feet, elbow and knee, and shoulder and hip. The three left cooperation include cooperation of left hand and right foot, left elbow and right knee, and left shoulder and right hip, which is similar to the right cooperation. In addition, the cooperation of head and hand, hand and body, and body and footstep can be called external ones and the cooperation of liver and joints, spleen and muscles, lung and kidney and bone can be called internal ones. In brief, in case one moves, all move and one cooperates, all cooperate and all the internal organs and bones are involved in it.

7. 六进 Six Advances

既知三合，犹有六进。夫六进者何也？头为六阳之首，而为周身之主，五官百骸莫不体此为向背，头不可不进也。手为先锋，根基在脚，脚不进，则手却不前矣，是脚亦不可不进也。气聚于腕，机关在腰，腰不进则气馁，而不实矣，此所以腰贵于进者也，意贯周身，运动在步，步不进而意则索然无能为矣；此所以必取其进也。以及上左必进右，上右必进左。共为六进，此六进者，孰非着力之地欤！要之：未及其进，合周身毫无关动之意，一言其进，统全体全无抽扯之形，六进之道如是而已。

Besides three cooperation, there are six advances. What are six advances? Head is the leader of Six *Yang* and owner of the entire body, and all the organs and bones listen to it, so head has to advance. Hand is the pioneer with the root of feet, and hand cannot go forward without feet advancing so feet have to advance. Breath is gathered in the wrist and is commanded at the waist, so breath will lose and become empty without waist advancing, which is even more important than advance. *Yi* is filled in the body, movement lies in footwork, and *Yi* will be incompetent without footstep advancing so footstep must advance. The other two advances include advancing right for going up to the left and advancing left for going up to the right. Why shall six advances be discussed? What is important is that failure of the advance means no sign of movement for the entire body and the emergence of advances means movements of the whole body.

8. 身法 Body Pose

夫发手击敌，全赖身法之助，身法维何？纵、横、高、低、进、退、反、侧而已。纵，则放其势，一往而不返。横，则理其力，开拓而莫阻。高，则扬其身，而身有增长之意。低，则抑其身，而身有攒促之形。当进则进，殚其力而勇往直前。当退则退，速其气而回转扶势。至于反身顾后，后即前也。侧顾左右，左右恶敢当我哉，而要非拘拘焉而为之也。察夫人之强弱，运乎已之机关，有忽纵而忽横，纵横因势而变迁，不可一概而推。有忽高而忽低，高低随时以转移，岂可执一而论。时而宜进不可退，退以馁其气。时而宜退，即以退，退以鼓其进。是进固进也，即退亦实以助其进。若反身顾后，而后不觉其为后。侧顾左右，而左右不觉其为左右。总之，观在眼，变化在心，而握其要者，则本诸身。身而前，则四体不命而行矣。身而怯，则百骸莫不冥然而处矣，身法顾可置而不论乎。

Body pose helps much in attacking the opponent. What is body pose? Vertical, horizontal, high, low, advancing, retreating, turnabout and turning aside. Vertical pose can make use of the position to go without returning. Horizontal pose can distribute the strength and explore without stop. High pose can raise the body and make the body tend to lengthen. Low pose can control the body and in case of advancing, use up the strength to go forward while in case of retreating, speed up the breath to return for proper position. As to turning around to take care of the back, the back is also the front and the side pose is to protect the right and left from the attack. And it is important to remember that they are not strictly defined. It is necessary to observe the strength and weakness of the opponent and make use of the chances and position to have sudden change of vertical and horizontal poses. And there is sudden change of high and low poses with time. In some cases, it is better to advance than retreat to avoid weaken the breath, and in other cases it is advisable to retreat to help advance, so advancing is advancing but retreating is in fact to help advance. In time of turnabout to protect the back, the back will no more be back and turning aside to protect the right and left, it is hard to see they are the right and left. In all, observation is made by eyes and change is by heart while the command is made by the body, if the body advances, its parts will follow naturally, but if the body fears, all the bones will be at loss. So the body pose is worth discussing here.

9. 步法 Footwork

今夫四肢百骸主于动，而实运以步；步者乃一身之根基，运动之枢纽也。以故应战，对战，本诸身。而所以为身之砥柱者，莫非步。随机应变在于手。而所以为手之转移者，又在于步。进退反侧，非步何以作鼓动之机？抑扬伸缩，非步何以示变化之妙？即谓观察在眼，变化在心，而转弯抹角，千变万化，不至穷迫者，何莫非步之司命，而要非勉强可致之也。动作出于无心，鼓舞出于不觉，身欲动而步以为之周旋，手将动而步亦早为之催迫，不期然而已然，莫之驱而若驱，所谓上欲动而下自随之，其斯之谓欤！且步分前后，有定位者，步也。无定位者，亦步也。如前步进，而后步亦随之，前后自有定位也。若前步作后步，后步作前步，更以前步作后步之前步，后步作前步之后步，前后亦自有定位矣。总之：捶以论势，而握要者步也。活与不活，在于步，灵与不灵亦在于步。步之为用大矣哉！

When all the limbs and bones are active, their application is shown in the footwork, which is the basis of the body and center of movement. Therefore, it is the footwork which is the backbone of the body to meet the attack, attack and control the body, and the hand is for change which can be transferred by footwork. How can advancing, retreating, turnabout and turning aside be made without the stimulus of footwork and how can rise and fall, extension and contraction show their wonderfulness without footwork? Though observation is by eyes and change is in heart, the footstep has the control of all the changes to avoid the awkward situation. It is a matter of course that, in case movement is not out of intention, and stimulus is not noticed, the footstep make preparation when the body tends to move and the footstep is leading when hands tend to move. Though it does not drive, it seems to drive, which is when the upper tends to move, the lower follows. In addition, footwork has the position of front and back and they can also have no positions. If the front footstep advances, the back footstep will follow, which means it has the positions of front and back. If the front footstep moves as the back one and the back as the front, the front footstep is the front footstep of the back one and the back footstep is the back footstep of the front one, thus there is also the position of front and back. In one word, position is introduced for discussing fist and the key part is the footstep. It is the footstep which accounts for flexibility and inflexibility, effectiveness and ineffectiveness, from which it can be seen that the footstep plays an important role.

10. 刚柔 Softness and Hardness

夫拳术之为用，气与势而已矣。然而气有强弱，势分刚柔，气强者取乎势之刚，气弱者取乎势之柔，刚者以千钧之力而扼百钧，柔者以百钧之力而破千钧，尚力尚巧，刚柔之所以分也。然刚柔既分，而发用亦自有别，四肢发动，气行诸外，而内持静重，刚势也。气屯于内，而外现轻和，柔势也。用刚不可无柔，无柔则环绕不速。用柔不可无刚，无刚则催逼不捷。刚柔相济，则粘、游、连、随、腾、闪、折、空、掤、捋、挤、按，无不得其自然矣。刚柔不可偏用，用武岂可忽耶。

Application of boxing technique is related to breath and momentum while the former may be strong or weak and the latter may be hard or soft, so the strong breath may use hard momentum and the weak use the soft. As a result, the hard controls one hundred pound strength by thousand pound strength while the soft controls one thousand pound strength by one hundred strength, which shows the art of focusing on strength or on skill and is the difference of the hard momentum and soft momentum. Since difference between hardness and softness has been shown, application of them shall be different. When the limbs moves, the breath walks outside and the inside is still, it is hard momentum, and when breath collects inside and the outside appearance is light, it is soft momentum. Application of hardness cannot lack softness otherwise it will turn round and become slow and application of softness cannot lack hardness otherwise stimulus will not be quick. Therefore, the mixed use of hardness and softness will make the movement natural: adhere, connect, stick, follow, jump, evade, bend, clear, ward-off, rollback, press and push. So neither of hardness nor softness shall be overstressed or overlooked in martial application.

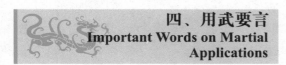

四、用武要言
Important Words on Martial Applications

要诀云：捶自心出，拳随意发，总要知己知彼，随机应变。

心气一发，四肢皆动，足起有地，动转有位，或粘而游，或连而随，或腾而闪，或折而空，或掤而挒，或挤而按。

拳打五尺以内，三尺以外，远不发肘，近不发手，无论前后左右，一步一捶，遇敌以得人为准，以不见形为妙。

拳术如战术，击其无备，袭其不意，乘击而袭，乘袭而击，虚而实之，实而虚之，避实击虚，取本求末，出遇众围，如生龙活虎之状，逢击单敌，似巨炮直轰之势。

上中下一气把定，身手足规距绳束，手不向空起，亦不向空落，精敏神巧全在活。

古人云：能去，能就，能刚，能柔，能进，能退，不动如山岳，难知如阴阳，无穷如天地，充实如太仓，浩渺如四海，眩耀如三光，察来势之机会，揣敌人之短长，静以待动，动以处静，然后可言拳术也。

要诀云：借法容易，上法难，还是上法最为先。

战斗篇云：击手勇猛，不当击梢，迎面取中堂，抢上抢下势如虎，类似鹰鹞下鸡场；翻江拔海不须忙，丹凤朝阳最为强；云背日月天交地，武艺相争见短长。

要诀云：发步进入须进身，身手齐到是为真，法中有诀从何取，解开其理妙如神。

古有闪进打顾之法：何为闪？何为进？进即闪，闪即进，不必远求。何为打？何为顾？顾即打，打即顾，发手便是。

古人云：心如火药，手如弹。灵机一动，鸟难逃。身似弓弦手似箭，弦响鸟落显奇神。起手如闪电，电闪不及合眸。击敌如迅雷，雷发不及掩耳。左过右来，右过左来；手从心内发，落向前落。力从足上起，足起犹火作。

上左须进右，上右须进左，发步时足根先着地，十趾要抓地，步要稳当，身要庄重，去时撒手，着人成拳，上下气要均停，出入以身为主宰；不贪，不欠，不即，不离。拳由心发，以身催手，一肢动百骸皆随；一屈，统身皆屈；一伸，统身皆伸；伸要伸得尽，屈要屈得紧。如卷炮卷得紧，崩得有力。

战斗篇云：不拘提打，按打，击打，冲打，膊打，肘打，胯打、腿打，头打，手打，高打，低打，顺打，横打，进步打，退步打，截气打，借气打，以及上下百般打法，总要一气相贯。

出身先占巧地，是为战斗要诀。骨节要对，不对则无力。手把要灵，不灵则生变。发手要快，不快则迟误。打手要狠，不狠则不济。脚手要活，不活则担险。存心要精，不精则受愚。

发身：要鹰扬猛勇，泼皮胆大，机智连环。勿畏惧迟疑；如关临白马，赵临长坂，神威凛凛，波开浪裂，静如山岳，动如雷发。

要诀云：人之来势，务要审察，足踢头前，拳打膊乍，侧身进步，伏身起发。

足来提膝，拳来肘拨；顺来横击，横来捧压；左来右接，右来左迎；远便上手，近便用肘；远便足踢，近便加膝。

拳打上风，审顾地形，手要急，足要轻，察势如猫行。心要整，且要清，身手齐到始成功。手到身不到，击敌不得妙。手到身亦到，破敌如摧草。

战斗篇云：善击者，先看步位，后下手势。上打咽喉下打阴，左右两肋并中心。前打一丈不为远，近打只在一寸间。

要诀云：操演时面前如有人，对敌时有人如无人。面前手来不见手，胸前肘来不见肘。手起足要落，足落手要起。

心要占先，意要胜人，身要攻人，步要过人，头须仰起，胸须现起，腰须竖起，丹田须运起，自项至足，一气相贯。

战斗篇云：胆战心寒者，必不能取胜。不能察形势者，必不能防入。

先动为师，后动为弟，能教一思进，莫教一思退。胆欲大而心欲小，运用之妙，存乎一心而已。一而运乎二气。行乎三节，现乎四梢，统乎五行。时时操演，朝朝运化，始而勉强，久而自然。拳术之道学，终于此而已矣。

Important formula says: Hammer (fist) comes from heart (mind). Fist follows Intention (*Yi*), generally one should know himself and the opponent, adapt to changing conditions.

Once heart and breath (*Qi*) emit, four extremities should move, legs rise (move) to a certain place, move and turn to a certain position, either stick (*zhan*) and move together (*you*), connect (*lian*) and follow (*sui*), jump (*teng*) and dodge (*shan*), turn over (*zhe*) and leave empty (*kong*), ward (*peng*) and roll (*lu*), push (*ji*) and press down (*na*).

Fist strikes within five feet but beyond three feet, too far means no use of elbow, too close means no use of hand, no matter whether you move forward or backward, to the left or right, one step one strike, when you meet opponent, catching him is the critria, not showing the shape (of your strike) is the excellence.

Fist method is like military tactics, attack where he is not prepared, hit where he has no intention, take advantage of attack and hit, take advantage of hitting and attack. First show the insubstantial (*Xu*) and then make the substantial (*Shi*), first it is substantial and then change to the insubstantial, avoid the substantial and attack the insubstantial, take root when you ask for branch. If you meet multiple opponents who surround you, appear strong like a living dragon or tiger, (then) attack one opponent, with a power of big cannon booming straight.

Top, middle and bottom should be handled by one Breath (*Qi*), body, hands and legs move according to established practice as is bound by a rope, hand should not rise empty neither fall empty, the sensitivity of the spirit is completely in agility.

The ancient people said: good at moving out and coming back, hardness and softness, moving forward and backward, when he does not move, he is like a mountain, difficult to know as *Yin* and *Yang*, limitless like heaven and earth, full and substantial like a granary, vast like four seas, dazzling like three lights, watching the coming force to find opportunity, able to estimate advantages and disadvantages of the opponent, awaiting movement of the opponent with stillness, handling stillness with movement, only if the above conditions are met one can talk about real boxing method.

Important formula says: method of borrowing opponent's power is easy, method of advancing is difficult, yet method of advancing is the most principal.

Writings on tactics say: attacking hand should be bold and powerful, do not attack the extremities, facing the opponent to take his middle hall (e.g. between the legs), like a tiger grab the upper part of his body or grab the lower, same to eagle or hawk capturing chicken from above; one does not have to hurry in overturning rivers and seas, the most powerful is Red Phoenix Facing Sun; clouds flow in the light of sun and moon heaven meets earth, only when two martial arts fight one with the other one can see weak and strong sides.

Important formula says: taking a step and entering one must advance body, the movement is real only if body and hands arrive together, in the method there is a formula about where to get it from.Once you understand this principle, you will realize how miraculous it is.

From ancient times there were methods of dodging (*shan*), advancing (*jin*), striking (*da*) and protecting (*gu*): What is called dodging? What is called advancing? Advancing is dodging. Dodging is advancing. There is no need to seek it far away. What is called striking? What is called protecting? Protecting is striking. Striking is protecting. Just a hand movement.

The ancient people said: heart (mind) is like gunpowder, hands are like bullets. To have a brainwave (sudden inspiration) and bird will not escape easily. Body is like bowstring, and hands like arrows. Bowstring sounds and bird falls down, which shows miraculous skill of the archer. Rise hands fast like flash of lightning, there is no time even to close eyes when lightning flashes. Strike the opponent like rapid thunder, there is no time to cover ears when thunder strikes.

Move to the left and come from the right, move to the right and come from the left; hands hit from inside of the heart, then fall forward. Strength rises from feet; feet rise just like fire does.

If you want to advance the left you should first enter right, while advancing the right , enter left, taking step heel first touches ground, ten toes should grasp ground, steps should be steady, body should be serious, when moving out withdraw hands, when reaching the opponent hands should clench into fists, upper and lower breath should all stop, in coming out and entering body should dominate; no deficiency, no shortage, no reaching, no leaving. Fist strikes from heart, hands are hastened by body, one extremity moves (and) one hundred (e.g. all) bones follow; once you bend (close), whole body also bends; once you extend open, whole body should also extend; extending should be to the limit, bending should be tight. It is like loading a cannon, the tighter it is loaded, the more power the explosion has.

Writings on tactics say: with restrictions or not; if you strike using lifting (*ti*), pressing (*an*), attacking (*ji*), pounding (*chong*), arms (*bo*), elbows (*zhou*), hips (*kua*), legs (*tui*), head (*tou*), hands (*shou*), (hit) high (*gao*), low (*di*), along (*shun*), horizontally (*heng*), with step forward (*jinbu*), with step backward (*tuibu*), borrowing breath (*jieqi*), stopping Qi (*jieqi*) as well as with hundreds of methods of striking up and down, generally speaking,all body should form one coherent whole literally—be penetrated by one breath.

Moving body first to take clever (e.g. favourable) place (position), this is called important formula of tactics. Joints of bones should be adjusted (*dui*), otherwise there is no strength. Hands should grasp with agility, otherwise situation may change unexpectedly (literally-change will be born). Hands should move (*issue*) fast, otherwise they will be delayed. Be ferocious when striking, otherwise the strike is of no benefit. Feet and hands must be alive, otherwise one will face danger. Cherish perfectly intentions (*cunxin*), otherwise you will be fooled.

Issuing with body should be fierce and courageous like raising eagle, in rude and brave style, quick-wits and wisdom should be linked. Do not fear and hesitate; like Guan Yu at Baima, Zhao Yun at Changban, awe-inspiring with invincible might, breaking waves, in stillness like a mountain, in movement like a thunder.

Important formula says: make sure to examine the coming movement of the opponent, how he kicks with legs and advances with head, strikes with fists and spread his arms, step forward with your side to the opponent, first bend body then rise and hit.

When leg arrives (e.g. opponent kicks) lift your knee, if fist arrives move it aside (*bo*) with elbow, attack horizontally (*heng*), if the opponent strikes straight (*shun*), ward off (*peng*) and press down (*ya*) a horizontal attack, receive the attack coming from the left with your right, meet the attack coming from the right with your left, on long distance use hand, on short distance use elbow, on long distance kick, on short distance add (use) knee.

If one wants to get upper hand in fighting, look around and examine the shape of ground around you, hands must be fast (*ji*), feet light (*qing*), examine the opponent's movements like a cat, heart (*mind*) must be in order and clear, when body and hands arrive at the target together this is the beginning of success. If hands arrive and the body does not, then this is striking without excellence. If hands arrive and body also arrives (at the same time), then defeating opponent is like smashing a weed.

Writings on tactics say: those good at fighting, first look at the opponent's footwork and only then strike with hands. High strike throat, low strike groin. Left and right ribs as well as center line. While advancing striking on the distance of one *zhang* (e.g. 3.33m) is not considered far, striking in close range is within one *chun*.

Important formula says: practice as if there was opponent in front of you, when facing opponent although there is opponent, but fight as if there was nobody. If a hand comes in front of your face do not look at it, if elbow comes in front of your chest do not look at it. When hands rise (*qi*), feet should fall (*luo*); when feet fall, hands should rise.

Heart (mind) must take the lead, intention (*yi*) must conquer the opponent, body must attack him, steps must pass through him, head must look up (*yang*), chest must be present (*xian*), waist must be upright (*shu*), Dantian must move (*yun*), body from feet to neck must be one coherent whole.

Writings on tactics say: those terrified will never achieve victory. Those who cannot examine situation will never protect (themselves).

Moving first (e.g. before the opponent) is called master, moving later (e.g. after the opponent) is called younger brother, teach to advance but not to retreat. Bold but cautious, secrets of movements and applications, everything is simply in one heart (mind). One moves into two energies (*qi*), transmitts to three parts (*jie*), appears in four tips (*shao*), unites in five elements (*wuxing*). Practice all the time, move and transform everyday, it is difficult at the beginning but becomes natural after a long time. Philosophy of fist art ends here.

第三节
陈氏太极拳历代传承简介
THE MAIN LINES OF TRANSMISSION
OF CHEN-STYLE TIJIQUAN

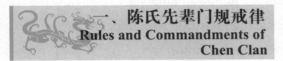

一、陈氏先辈门规戒律
Rules and Commandments of Chen Clan

1. 门尊十二严 Twelve Strictness

端 （举止端正庄重）
Duan (dignified manners)

敬 恭敬尊重
Jing (respectful)

公 公正
Gong (fair)

正 正直、正派
Zheng (honest and upright)

仁 仁慈、善良
Ren (benevolent, kind)

义 正义
Yi (just, righteous)

浩 浩然之气、胸怀宽
Hao (noble spirit, broad-minded)

勇 见义勇为
Yong (having the courage to do what is right)

忠 忠诚老实
Zhong (loyal)

信 信仰、崇拜
Xin (belief, worship)

诚 诚心诚意
Cheng (earnestly and sincerely)

德 品德、道德
De (morality, ethics)

2. 规守甘备 Advice and Warning

（1）不倚权欺人。Do not bully on one's power.

（2）不畏强凌弱。Do not fear the strong and bully the weak.

（3）不惧险、救危。Do not fear danger but help the distressed.

（4）不为非作歹。Do not commit any crime.

（5）不仗技采花。Do not choose beauty on the skills.

（6）不借势狂妄。Do not be impetuous.

（7）不走街卖艺。Do not become a street-performer.

（8）不串乡结党。Do not band together.

（9）不奢逸流浪。Do not tramp for comfort.

（10）不自骄自满。Do not be conceited.

（11）不与狂徒较量。Do not confront with impetuous people.

（12）不与无知争强。Do not prove the ability with the ignorant.

（13）不可骄谄贫富。Do not fawn on the rich and humiliate the poor.

（14）不贪无义横财。Do not covet ill-gotten wealth.

（15）不过酒色处事。Do not have sensual pursuits.

（16）不抗公私之债。Do not protest the private and public debts.

（17）不得损公碍私。Do not harm the public and the individual.

（18）不图显官厚禄。Do not pursue high position with high pay.

（19）不当叛国臭徒。Do not be a shameful traitor.

（20）不应蹉懈习攀。Do not waste time progress.

3. 戒章十二禁 Twelve Bans

邪　不正当的事（歪风邪气）

Xie (not proper things; unhealthy trends and evil practice)

反　坏，恶（指坏人坏事，为非作歹）

Fan (*Huai, e*; bad people and wrong deeds, commit crimes)

刁　无赖

Diao (rascally)

猾　狡猾

Hua (cunning, tricky)

奢　过分奢侈、挥霍

She (too luxurious, wasteful)

诈　欺诈，诓骗

Zha (cheat, deceive)

疯　言行狂妄

Feng (impetuous in words and deeds)

卑　下贱、品质低劣

Bei (degrading, low morality)

奸　奸诈、虚伪、背叛、下流、不老实

Jian (treacherous, hypocritical, dishonest)

狂　极端任性、狂妄、妄自尊大

Kuang (extremely willful, overweening)

恶　恶毒、凶狠、极坏行为

E　(vicious, malicious, extremely bad deeds)

4. 律则二格　Two Maxims for Commandment

（1）善良之人，端德者习拳，以强身健体为身之本，此乃陈门拳术本貌共遵。

For kind people they practice Taiji with morality to build the body for health, which follows the original purpose of Chen style Taiji.

（2）不良之人，邪恶者从拳、以资侮掠人致本，为患害。此乃陈门拳术戒绝反对。

For evil people, they become stronger with ill intention to bully and loot ,which is severely condemned by Chen style Taiji.

5. 学拳须知　Notice for Taiji Practice

学太极拳不可不敬，不敬则外慢师友，内慢身体，心不敛束，何能学艺？

学太极拳不可狂，狂则生是非。不但手不可狂，言亦不可狂，外面形迹必带儒雅风气，不然狂于外，必失于中。

学太极不可满，满则招损。俗语云："天外有天，人外有人。"能谦则虚必受教，人岂不乐告之以善哉？积众以为善，善思大矣。

学太极拳当细心揣摩，一招不揣摩，则此势机智情理终于茫昧，即承上启下处，尤当留心，此处不留心，则来脉不真，转换不灵，动一式自成一招，不能自始至终一气贯通矣，不能一气贯通，则与太和元气终难问津。

学太极拳先学读书，书理明白，学拳自然容易。

It is hard to practice Taijiquan without respect, as lack of respect will lead to the impoliteness to teachers and friends outside and carelessness to the body inside, and how can one practice Taiji without restraint of heart?

It's not right to be impetuous for Taijiquan practice, as impetuosity leads to troubles; both hands and words shall not be impetuous while the air of Confucian elegance is expected, as the impetuosity outside means the loss inside.

It's not right to be conceited for Taijiquan practice, as conceit invites disaster. The saying goes, "there are heavens beyond heaven, there are experts besides the expert."

If one can be modest, one will learn much from others who are ready to tell him the good, based on which one can become open-minded. It will be helpful to try to fathom carefully for Taijiquan practice. In case one form is not figured out, the wisdom and law of the posture will end up obscure. Special attention is needed for the form of connecting links, otherwise it will lead to the false source ineffective change, independent movements and failure to thread together from beginning to end which makes *Taihe* vitality beyond reach.

Read books before studying Taijiquan, as it is easy to study with the knowledge of its theory.

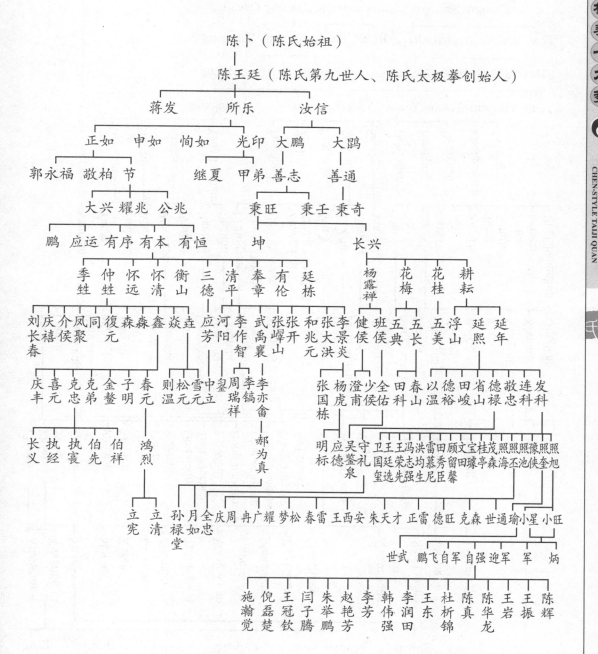

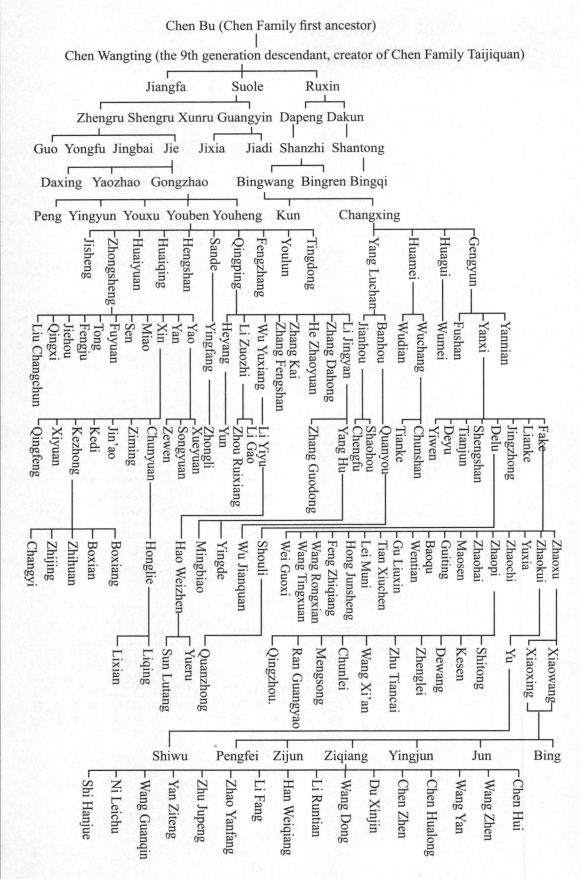

Chen Bu (Chen Family first ancestor)

Chen Wangting (the 9th generation descendant, creator of Chen Family Taijiquan)

第四节
陈氏太极拳对身体各部位的要求
CHEN-STYLE TAIJIQUAN'S REQUIREMENT ON EVERY PART OF HUMAN BODY

谚云："不以规矩，不能成方圆。"陈氏太极拳对周身各个部位都有严格要求。

A saying goes, "No rules, no standards." Chen Family Taijiquan has strict requirements on every part of human body.

一、头颈部
Requirement on Head and Neck

《十大要论》、《拳经》、《拳论》中说："头为六阳之首、周身之主，五官百骸莫不体此为向背。"拳论规定："百会穴领共全身"，"自始自终顶劲决不可失"。还有"虚灵顶劲"、"提顶"、"吊顶"、"头顶悬"等说法。所以用领、提、虚、灵等字来描绘头颈部位，主要是怕中气过于上冲，从而引起颈部肌肉僵直，失掉头部的灵活性，导致全身的僵滞。

从力学上讲，头处在人体上下垂直竖线上，从生理学来讲，头部的大脑是神经系统的中枢。如果练拳时头部东倒西歪，势必影响身体的平衡和协调，不但失去动作姿势的优美，也影响精神的集中。《拳论》说："腰脊为第一主宰，喉头为第二主宰。"练拳时，头颈部要领掌握得好，才能使精神集中。一招一势，举手投足，受着意识的指导；动作起来，才能像拳经中所讲的周身灵活。否则就显得精神涣散，动作失去完整和协调。"一失顶劲，四肢若无所附，且无精神。故必领起，以为周身纲领。"

具体要求是：头部要保持正直，颈部肌肉要保持松弛状态，使头部有悬起的感觉。注意不要勉强和呆板，避免前俯后仰、东倒西歪。身体移动和旋转时，头颈部与身躯四肢要上下一致，两目要平视延远。运行中，目手为主，眼神注于该手的中指端。下颚要微向内收，牙齿和口唇要微合。舌尖抵住上腭，以加强唾液分泌。耳听身后，兼顾左右。总之，处处要自然轻松，不可有丝毫急躁的情绪。

The books *Ten Main Theories*, *Quan Jing* (Treatise on Taijiquan) and *Quan Lun* (Theories on Taijiquan) say that head is the leading part of Six Positives (*Yang*, according to traditional Chinese medicine's theory, Six *Yangs* include three veins in hand and three veins in foot. These six veins get together on head, so head is called as leading part of six *Yangs*) and the master of body. Five organs (referring to eyes, ears, mouth, nose and tongue) and all bones conduct as head indicates. *Quan Lun* says that *Baihui* Acupoint is the point where breath (*qi*) and blood get together, and that breath (*qi*) on head should never be leaked all along. There is another says such as relaxation producing energy, raise head, hang head and dangle head. So using lead, raise, empty and relax to describe head and neck, it is mainly because body become stiff and rigid if Middle Breath (*qi*) is uprising too fast, resulting muscle around neck to be stiff and head's flexibility will lose.

From the view-point of science of mechanics, the head locates on the vertical line of the body. From the view-point of physiology, the brain is the centrums of nervous system. If head swings and dangles when practicing Taijiquan, balance and coordination of body shall be impacted severely, which results in no beauty of posture and no spiritual concentration. *Quan Lun* says that backbone is the most important part and throat is the second important one. When practicing Taijiquan, head and neck should be mastered well. In this way, spirit can be concentrated. Every action and posture shall be guided by consciousness. Practice can make each part of body flexible. Otherwise, performance seems loose, disorganized and uncompleted. So some experts say that once head energy is lost, arms and legs has nothing to guide their action and people will feel fatigue, so head should be raised and guide the action of every part of whole body.

Specific requirements: head keeps straight. Muscle around neck keeps loose and relaxed. Head feels hanged up. Attention not to be forced. Avoid bowing forward and leaning backward, reeling or lurching. When body moves and spins, head and neck should keep harmonious with body. Eyes see at its level and into far away. During practicing, one hand is as a guider and sight should be concentrated on tip of middle finger. Chin should pull back to body slightly. Teeth and lip should be close naturally. Tip of tongue raises against palate so as to speed up secretion of saliva. Ear listens and concentrates around. In one word, be natural and loose and don't have any impatient motion.

二、躯干部
Body

躯干部指的是人体的胸背、腰脊、腹部和臀部。这些部位是人体内脏所在和内脏的保护性支架，在健身、防身和技击等方面起着重要的作用。

Body here refers to chest, back, backbone, stomach and butt. These parts are where abdominal organs locate and are the protection framework of them. They play very important roles in body building, self-protection and skilled attacking, etc.

1. 胸背 The Chest and Back

陈氏太极拳对胸部的要求是要含、要虚，要松。拳经中说："胸要含住劲，又要虚。""胸间松开，胸一松，全体舒畅。"胸部含虚和胸间松开，可以自然形成腹式呼吸，使呼吸深长舒畅。从技击意义上讲，胸部虚含，锁骨和肋骨松沉，可以使上肢虚灵和身体重心向下降，有助于"紧要全在胸中腰间运化"。

对背部的要求是要舒展松沉，"用中气贯注"。人体背部呈微弧形，有脊椎骨上下连接，是脊髓神经所在部位。按照经络学说，背部是督脉的通道，督脉则属阳脉之海。练拳时，背部肌肉要注意舒展和向下松沉，要根据脊椎生理状态，随屈就伸，保持脊背的相对端正，以利于气血的通畅，做到"牵动往来气贴背"，便于及时使"力由脊发"。有的学派对背部提出了"拔背"的要求，我认为用这个"拔"字，容易使人产生误解，就字义讲，"拔"是向上提拔的意思。人体脊背部不论是上拔还是前屈，都会使背阔肌和肋间肌拉紧前伸，迫使胸部向内吞缩，两肩前扣，形成弓背耸肩的不良姿势，既影响和破坏身法的优美，又使胸腔受到一定压迫，妨碍呼吸的顺畅。

Chen Family Taijiquan's requirements on chest is to tighten up the belly, harbour chest, and keep loose and relaxed. *Quan Jing* says chest should harbour breath (*qi*) in it and keep relaxed, which can form the abdominal breathing and make breathing profound and ease. From the meanings of martial art, pulling back chest and loosening the clavicle and costa can make upper limbs agile and reduce the body's center of gravity. It's also benefit for "main breath (*qi*) is moving in the chest and waist".

Chen Family Taijiquan's requirements on back is to stretch out and relax, make middle breath (*qi*) in it. Human's back is arched, connected from upper to lower by vertebra. It's where spinal ganglion is. According to the theory of channels and collaterals, the back is the channel of *Du*, which belongs to *Yang* channel. When practicing Taijiquan, muscle around back should be loosen, sunk and relaxed, which keeps back in its own shape. This is benefit of breath (*qi*) and blood moving more freely, reaching that breath (*qi*) existing in back through moving and pushing, which is convenient for "power exploding from back at once". Some philosophical sects offer the requirement of "Pull Back" on back. I think that the word Pull will make people confused and understand wrong. From the surface meaning of "Pull", it means "Raise Up". No matter human body pulls up or bends forward, it always make latissimus dorsi and intercostal muscle become stressed, forcing chest to pull in and both shoulders to tension forward, which make people has harmful posture with bent back and hunch shoulders. It not only affects the graceful posture, but also presses the chest and affects breath freely.

2. 腰脊　Waist and Spine

人在日常生活中，行走坐卧，要保持正确的姿势，腰脊起着重要的作用。在练习太极拳的过程中，腰脊的作用更为重要。有"腰脊为第一主宰"的说法。陈氏太极拳对腰部的要求是：腰劲向下塌。就是腰部椎弓要按生理弯曲，略向内收下沉，向下塌住劲，腰是上下体转动的枢纽。在含胸的情况下，向下塌住劲，能够使心气下降，下盘稳固。同时，还要注意两肋微内收，即拳论中的"束肋"。但是腰劲下塌不可用力太过。在《拳经》的论著中，一方面说"腰劲贵下去，贵坚实"，另一方面说"腰中要虚，一虚则上下皆灵"。《拳经》中又说："腰为上下体枢纽转关处，不可软，亦不可硬，折其中方得。"如果腰部过于用力，会使腰大肌收缩，影响上下体转动的灵活性。

在塌腰的同时，还要注意使腰脊直竖，就是所谓"直腰"。成年人的脊柱由26块椎骨组成，由于直立的影响，从侧面看，有颈弯、胸弯、腰弯和骶弯四个生理弯曲，其中腰椎是向前弯曲的。又因为椎骨之间，有关节软骨和关节韧带相连接，活动性强，伸缩性大，容易受其他部位的肌肉牵引，而出现俯仰歪斜的现象。做好"直腰"，就是为了尽可能地减小腰弯的前曲度，避免在全身放松的情况下，影响脊椎的正常生理状态，维持立身中正，使腰脊更好地起到"车轴"的作用。《拳论》说："心为令，气为旗，腰为轴"，这里指的就是腰脊要像旗杆那样直竖着。需要说明的是，在练习过程中，腰椎以上的胸椎部分，根据动作的需要，有时虽然有些轻微的伸缩，但不可随意摇摆，要注意曲中求直。

In normal life, when people walk, sit and lie down, if you want to keep correct posture, the waist spine is important. In the process of practicing Taijiquan, the effect of waist spine is more important. It has the parlance that "waist spine is the first master". Chen Family Taijiquan requires that waist must lower down. It means that waist spine should bend according to physiological feature and then exert down to keep energy sink down. Waist is an essential part when upper and lower body move and turn around. When the chest sinks, keeping energy sinking down can reduce breath (*qi*) and make crura rocky. At the same time, you should pay attention that the ribs should be pulled inside, which is called "Tighten Rib". But when waist energy sinks, don't be too energetic. On one hand, *Quan Lun* says that it is precious for waist power to sink down and be firm. On the other hand, it says that waist need relaxed and relaxation makes body flexible. *Quan Jing* also says, "waist is the hinge of the upper and lower body. It should not be too soft or too hard. Waist can accomplish its function only when keeping middle." If waist moves too energetic, the muscle of waist will shrink and also the flexibility of upper and lower body will be impacted.

At the time when waist sinks, pay attention to keep backbone straight. This is called "Waist Upright". Adult's backbone is consisting of 26 vertebras. With the effect of waist upright, viewing from one side, the body appears four bendings, which is neck bending, chest bending, waist bending and hipbone bending, among which waist is bending forward. Because there is joint-cartilage and ligament-cartilage connecting the vertebrae together, backbone has strong flexibility and good stretching, so it is easy to be pulled by other muscle and the phenomenon of crouching, facing-upward, bending and slanting happens. Doing "waist upright" well is to minimize bending degree of curvature of waist and to avoid bringing any influence to normal physiological status when relaxing body so as to keep body straight and make waist fulfill its function. *Quan Lun* says that heart is commander, breath (*qi*) is the flag and waist is the main axis. This sentence means that waist is upright as a flag. One thing that needs to interpret is when practicing Taijiquan, the thoracic vertebra which is located upper of waist will slightly extend and shorten. But the thoracic vertebra cannot freely swing, practioner should pay attention to keeping upright when bending.

3. 腹部 Abdomen

　　陈氏太极拳对腹部的要求是要"合"。《拳论》中说："中间胸腹，自天突穴至脐下阴交、气海，石门、关元如磬折，如鞠躬形，是谓含住胸，是为合住劲，要虚。"又说："胸腹宽宏广大，向前合住，中气贯注。"腹部是丹田所在的地方，丹田是中气归宿的场所。练习太极拳时，周身之劲，往外发者，皆起于丹田。腹肋的左右气冲、维道穴向气海，关元、巾极虚虚合住，有利于中气出入丹田，有利任脉的通畅。有的太极拳家提出"腹松"；有的提出"空胸实腹"。实际上，腹部肌肉随着中气出入丹田有张有弛，两者并不矛盾，是"中气存于中，虚灵含于内"。

Chen Family Taijiquan's requirement on abdomen is to sink and close. *Quan Lun* says that chest connects with abdomen through *Tiantu* Acupoint to lower of bellybutton. *Shimen* Acupoint and *Guanyuan* Acupoint are like breaking rocks and appear a bowing posture. This is called wrapping the upper chest, keep body energetic and relaxed. It also says that chest and abdomen is wide and big and breath (*qi*) can be contained in them. Abdomen is where *Dantian* Acupoint locates. *Dantian* Acupoint is the place where Middle Breath (*qi*) gets together. When practicing Taijiquan, energy over the bodies which can be used are all from *Dantian* Acupoint. The Middle Breath (*qi*) from *Qichong* Acupoint on both sides and *Weidao* Acupoint get together with breath (*qi*) from *Qihai* Acupoint, *Guanyuan* Acupoint and *Jinji* Acupoint, which is benefit that Middle Breath (*qi*) easily enter and exit from *Diantian* Acupoint, and also benefit flood flows in the *Renmai* veins. Some Taijiquan experts propose "abdomen keeps relaxed" and some propose "empty chest and solid abdomen". But in fact, the abdominal muscle should be tensive and relaxed when the Middle Breath (*qi*) enters the *Dantian* Acupoint. There is no contradiction between tension and relaxation. It means that Middle Breath (*qi*) exists in *Dantian* and the same as spiritual energy.

4. 臀部 Buttocks

陈氏太极拳对臀部的要求是要"泛"。在《拳经》中，曾多次提出臀部要"泛起"，要"翻起"。《拳经》中又说："屁股泛不起来，不惟前裆合不住，即上体亦皆扣合不住。"在塌腰、合腹、开胯、圆裆的配合下，臀部向后微泛，有利中气贯于脊中；有利于腰劲、裆劲、腿劲的运用。泛臀绝不是撅屁股，不是突臀。泛臀是塌腰、合腹、圆裆、开胯、合膝的必然结果。"前裆合住，后臀自然翻起。"有的太极学派提出了"敛臀"，就是臀部微向里收的要求。敛臀固然可以防止撅屁股的毛病，但是，如果只注意臀部向里收敛，则前裆大开，后裆夹住，裆劲不能开圆，就会影响身体转动的灵活性。

Chen Family Taijiquan's requirement on buttocks is to rise slightly and backward. *Quan Jing* repeats that buttocks should be raised slightly and backward. *Quan Jing* also says, "If buttock does not rise slightly and backward, crotch of human body can not close, that means that upper body can not close too." Under the cooperation of sinking waist, closing abdomen, opening buttocks and circling crotch, buttock rises backward slightly, which benefits that Middle Breath (*qi*) goes through backbone and energy from waist, crotch and leg can fulfill its function. Buttock Rise definitely does not mean to lift or extrude. Buttock Rise is the inevitable result after lowering waist, closing abdomen, circling crotch and close beneath. "Front crotch closes and back buttock naturally rises." Some Taijiquan specialist proposes Withdraw Buttock, referring to that buttock withdraws slightly. Withdrawing buttock surely can prevent buttock extruding outward, but if practicer just pays attention to withdrawing buttock, simultaneously making front crotch open and back crotch close tightly which results in crotch energy can not break out, body flexibility shall be influenced.

三、上肢部
Arms

1. 肩肘 Shoulder and Elbow

"松肩沉肘"是各派太极拳的共同要求。有的也叫"沉肩垂肘"或

"沉肩坠肘"，就是两肩关节要向下向外松开，两肘关节要向下沉坠。松肩和沉肘是相互联系的。只有做到沉肘松肩，两臂才能圆满松活，运动自然。《拳论》讲："转关在肩，折叠在腕。"也就是说，解脱擒拿，内劲运动在胸腰。通过肩肘，力达手腕，方能解脱。肩肘关节的通顺，内劲才能达到掌指。如果肩肘受到障碍，便会影响内劲运用，从而影响到周身协调。在练习时，经常要注意两肩关节的松弛，有意识地向外引伸，使劲逐渐拉开下沉；两肘则要有下垂之意，以起到"护肋"的作用。同时，还要注意使腋下留有大约一个拳头的空隙，以利于手臂的旋转自如。肩臂的上下左右旋转，虽然要求轻灵，但不可漂浮和软化。处处要力争圆满，做到轻而不浮，沉而不僵。但是这种功夫必须日久才能达到。《拳经》中说："肩膊头骨缝要开。始则不开，不可使之强开。功夫未到自开时，心说已开，究竟未开。必功苦日久，自然能开，方算得开。此处一开，则全胳膊之往来屈伸，如风吹杨柳，天机动荡，活泼泼地毫无滞机，皆系于此。此肱之枢纽，灵动所关，不可不知。"

To loosen shoulder and sink elbow are the same requirements by all Taijiquan specialists. Some experts call it as "Sink Shoulder and Droop Elbow". That means shoulder joint should loose backward and elbow joint should droop naturally. Loosen Shoulder and Sink Elbow has close relationship. Only when shoulder is loose and elbow is sinking, can arms practice freely and naturally. *Quan Lun* says that turning joint depends on shoulder and folding lies on wrist. That means, getting rid of arrest, usage of inner energy depends on chest and waist. Along with shoulder and elbow, power can reach wrist so as to get rid of arrest. Inner energy can reach to finger tip when shoulder and elbow move smoothly. If shoulder and elbow is strained, inner energy shall be impact so that coordination of body part shall be influenced. When practicing, pay more attention to the loosing of two shoulder joints and consciously to stretching outward, making energy sink. Elbow should sink, which can play a role to protect rib. At the same time, pay attention to leaving a space under armpit in which a fist can be put in so as to make arms move freely and randomly. Though it is required that shoulder and arms move freely and randomly, it should be flexible and fragile, not floating or soften. Every movement should be achieved perfect. To achieve this needs time. *Quan Jing* says that shoulder joint should be open. When starting practice, it is definitely not open, but it should not be forced to open. As practice goes on, it will naturally open. That is called Naturally Open. When it opens, arms can move randomly, like willow trees dancing in wind. Elbow is the essential part of arm and movement of arms depends on it. It should be know by every practicer.

2. 腕 Wrist

陈氏太极拳有竖腕、坐腕、折腕、旋转腕等多种变化，是随着动作的需要、身法的协调而变化的。如搂膝、懒扎衣、单鞭等势，手掌都应竖腕；掩手肱拳、云手、当头炮等势应直腕；抱头推山、六封四闭等势应坐腕；懒扎衣转六封四闭和高探马下边的过渡动作、三换掌等势，应折叠腕；六封四闭前边的过渡动作、倒卷肱转换动作等势，应旋转腕。但是，不论千变万化，必须结合身法，以中气运行而变化之。既要使腕部灵活多变，又要使腕部具有一定的柔韧性。绝不可为了花哨好看而变为浮漂软化，失去腕部的掤劲，这样在推手时就容易被对方拿住手腕而受制。

Chen Family Taijiquan has vertical wrist, horizontal wrist, folding wrist, revolving wrist and so on. As requested by movement, body changes. Palm should be vertically closed in the action of brush knee, Lazy about Tying Coat (In ancient China, when fighting with each other, people will tuck their long sleeves to make them comfortable.), single whip and so on. Hand should be Straight Wrist in the action of Covered Hand Punch, Cloud Hand, Cannon Overhead, etc. Hand should be Sitting Wrist in the action of Embrace Head & Push Mountain and Six Sealing & Four Closing. Hand should be Overlap Wrist in the difficult action of Lazy about Tying Coat changing into Six Sealing & Four Closing, High Pat on Horse, and so on. Hand should be Turning Wrist in the transition moves before starting Six Sealing & Four Closing and in the moves of Step Back Whirling Arms. But, whatever moves changes, moves must combine with body action, making Middle Breath (*qi*) run and move change. Taijiquan can make wrist agile but also can make wrist has certain flexibility. It is undesirable for Taiji practioners to chasing beauty of posture instead of losing agility of wrist. Otherwise, it is easy to be arrested when pushing hand.

3. 手 Hand

陈氏太极拳很重视手的作用。《拳论》说："此艺全是以心运手，以手领肘，以肘领身。" "每一举一动，其运化在身，表现在手。"又有"梢节领(手为梢节)，中节随，根节催"之说。从手型上讲，主要有掌、拳、钩三种。下面分别论之。

Chen Family Taijiquan focuses on the function of hand. *Quan Lun* says that this martial art is to run hand with heart, to lead elbow by hand and activate body by elbow. It also says that every move and action runs in body and show through hand. There is another says that tip (refering to hand) is as a leader, elbow is as the follower and body as a pusher. Hand style is classified into palm, fist and hook. The details shall be described as follows.

（1）掌 (Palm) 陈氏太极拳对掌的要求是瓦拢掌。就是拇指与小指有相合之意，中指、食指、无名指微向后仰。五指均轻微合拢，但不可用力，掌心要虚。有的拳家主张"三空"，即掌心空、脚心空、心空。但这不是绝对的，在拳式的运动中也会有变化。如在运动与合劲时，掌心要虚；在开劲与发劲时，掌心就要实。

另外，陈氏太极拳的缠丝劲有顺有逆，在手上的表现也有所不同。如在做逆缠丝时，拇指领劲向外按(如：六封四闭为左右双逆缠)，内劲由拇指到食指，到中指，依次贯足指梢；在做顺缠丝时，小指领劲向里合(如：运手一势往里合劲时，皆为顺缠，往外开时皆为逆缠)，由小指到无名指到中指，一直合于拇指，都是随着手臂的旋转依次贯注指肚，也就是力达指梢。只是陈氏太极拳在运行中除随着身法与手臂的旋转依次贯注指肚外，思想意识与眼神都是贯注于中指。拳论中说："中指劲到，余指劲也到。"

Chen Family Taijiquan's palm posture is called as Spade Trowel Hand. It refers to thumb closing to little finger and middle finger, forefinger and ring finger slightly rise backward. All five fingers gather together slightly but should not push any strength. The center of palm shall keep empty. Some practiser insists Three Empty, which refers to Palm Empty, Food's Center Empty and Heart Empty. But it is not absolute. During moving palms, hand style has some changes. When people practice and concentrate energy, center of palm should be empty. When opening energy and use it, center of palm should be solid.

In addition, Chen Family Taijiquan's Wrapping Jin is in sequence or against sequence and what is shown on hand is different. When doing inverse wrapping, thumb guides energy push outward (for example, Six Sealing & Four Closing is about double reverse bound). Inner energy is from thumb to forefinger and then to middle finger. When doing positive wrapping, little finger leads energy inward (for example, when Moving Hand close inward, it is positive wrapping and when it closes outward, it should be inverse wrapping), from little finger to ring finger then to middle finger and the energy will get together on thumb. Energy will concentrate on pad of fingers in sequence. That means energy reaches end of finger. When practicing Chen Family Taijiquan, energy will run along the revolving of arms and concentrate on pad of fingers, but also sense of consciousness and eye are concentrating on middle finger. *Quan Lun* says that once energy reaches to middle finger, energy also reaches other fingers yet.

（2）拳 (Fist)　陈氏太极拳的握拳形式是以四指并拢卷曲，指尖贴于掌心，然后拇指弯曲，贴于食指与中指中节上，握成拳形，但又不能握得太紧。如握太紧，会使整个手臂与半侧身体肌肉的紧张度增加，呈现僵硬，内劲不能顺利达到拳顶。所以《拳论》有"蓄势散手，着人成拳"之说。也就是说：在蓄劲时要虚握拳，在发劲着人的一瞬间成拳，力贯拳顶。使劲由足而生，行于腿，主宰于腰，通过肩肘，达到拳顶，周身完整一气。但注意在发拳时，腕部千万不能软，拳顶不能上撩，也不能下栽，必须直腕。如腕部软塌，拳遇实物，就会受伤。

The way of fist of Chen Family Taijiquan is that four fingers close together and bend, make the fingertips in the center of palm, then bend pollex and close to points middle of forefinger and medium, make all the fingers to the shape of fist, but don't tighten. Fisting too tight will make the tensity of whole arm and half of body muscle increase, appearing stiff. Inner can't reach to tip of fist. So *Quan Lun* has said that "move starts from open palm and forms a fist when attack others". That's, the fist is empty in its center when accumulate energy and fist become solid at the time to fight others with energy concentrating on fist. Energy that produces from foot and runs along leg is led by waist and reachs the tip of fist through elbow joint. Thus energy is full of body. Pay attention that when attacking, wrist can't be soften, tip of fist should keep leveled. If wrist is soft and loose, fist will be hurt when encountering solid body.

（3）钩手 (Hook hand)　就是五指合拢，腕部钩住放松，不能形成死弯。如用力死钩，会使腕部与臂部僵直，失去灵活，阻碍经气的循行。钩手可以锻炼腕部的旋转，含有叼手、擒手与解脱擒拿的方法。在套路练习中，对钩手的动作意义不可忽视。

Hook hand means five fingers close together, wrist is like a hook and keep relaxed, it can't form dead bend. If hook with great energy, wrist and arm shall be stiff and lose their agility, preventing breath (*qi*)'s circulation. Hook Hand can practice the revolving of wrist. It includes the style of Pickup Hand, Arrest Hand and Get-rid-of-arrest, which cannot be neglected when practicing the moves of Hook Hand.

四、下肢部（腿部）
The Lower limbs (Legs)

下肢是支撑身体的根基和劲力发动的根源。《拳论》说："其根在脚，发于腿，主宰于腰，形于手指"，"有不得劲处，身便散乱，必至偏倚，其病必于腰腿求之"，"步为周身之枢纽，灵与不灵在于步，活与不活在于步"，都是讲腿步姿势动作的重要性。

Legs are the foundation to support body and the source of energy. *Quan Lun* says that the foundation exists in foot, originates from leg, guided by waist and forms onto fingers. It also says that the place where people feels uncomfortable, body will feel fatigue and posture looks unbalanced. It is estimated that the uncomforting must be from waist or legs. Stepping position is critical for body and agility or not depends on stepping. These all interpret the importance of stepping position and posture.

1. 裆 Crotch

陈式太极拳对裆部的要求是要圆、要虚、要松、要活，避免出现尖裆、塌裆和死裆。《拳论》说："肾囊两旁谓之裆，贵圆贵虚。"又说："裆内自有弹簧力，灵机一转鸟难飞。"裆在套路运行和技击方面都起着重要作用。

圆裆，就是两胯根与两膝盖要撑开、撑圆而又有相合之意。每逢开步时，一腿实，一腿虚，虚腿脚尖里扣，小腿肚和大腿肌（即股内斜肌）才有内旋外转之意，再加上会阴处的虚虚上提，裆部就有圆、虚之感，就可避免尖裆（人字裆）的虚实不分。松裆和活裆，就是胯节与臀部肌肉要放松，不能死顶住骨盆，虚实要灵活变换。裆部的虚实变换，不像挂钟一样左右摆动。左右变换时，走的足平行"∞"字，内外旋转；在前后变换时，走的是下弧线。这样才能避免"死裆"不动、虚实不分、只见上肢活动的现象。塌裆是臀部低于膝盖，膝关节有了死弯，步法不轻，犯了转关不灵的毛病。裆部的会阴穴是任、督二脉的起点，练拳时，头顶的百会穴与裆部的会阴穴上下呼应，阴阳经气得到平稳，也有利于立身中正。

在运动过程中，腰与裆有密切关系，裆与胯膝也要相互配合。腰能松沉，胯能撑开，膝能里合，裆劲自能撑圆。《太极拳经说》中说："下腰劲，尻微翻起，裆劲自然合住。"又说："尻骨，环跳撅起来，里边腿根撑开，裆自开；两膝合住，裆自然合。"

Chen Family Taijiquan requires that crotch should be roundish, relaxed, loose and agile. Avoid the extruding crotch, sinking crotch and closing crotch appearing. *Quan Lun* says that the organs on both sides of bladder are called crotch and more roundish and relaxed, more precious. It also says that there is spring force inside of crotch and even bird can not fly away from crotch. Crotch plays a very important role in running of a set martial arts and skilled attacking.

Roundish Crotch means roots of crotch and two knees should rise up and form a circle. When open stepping, one leg stands solidly and firmly and the other leg stands empty. The foot tip on empty leg stand inward, small calf and thigh muscle look as turning inward and overturning outward. Plus the perineum slowly rising, crotch will looks like a circle, which avoids crotch of extruding. Loose crotch is the muscle on hip and buttock should be relaxed and should not stand up to pelvis. Solid leg and empty leg shall change with each other. The transition from solidness to emptiness is not like a lock swing. When the action of right leg and left leg exchange with each other, stepping moves like "∞" and turns inward and outward. When exchanging front stepping and behind stepping, stepping moves a concaved line. This can avoid Dead Crotch unmoving, no clear different between solidness and emptiness and we only see arms are moving. Sink Crotch refers to that buttock is lower than knee. There is Dog Leg on knees joint. Stepping will be unnatural, which results in turning influenced. *Huiyin* Acupoint is the starting point of *Ren* vein and *Du* vein. When practicing Taijiquan, *Baihui* Acupoint on the top of head will call and repose to *Huiyin* Acupoint on crotch. *Yin* and *Yang* will be balanced and stable. It is also beneficial of body upright.

During practicing, waist and crotch has close relationship. Crotch will cooperate with hip and knee. Waist can sink, hip can open and knees can close inward. Crotch can become a circle naturally. *Taiji Classics* says to sink waist's energy and to raise end of spine slightly and then crotch can naturally close. It also says that spine bone rise, root of leg open, thus crotch naturally open and that two knees close and crotch naturally close.

2. 胯（髋） Hip

陈式太极拳对胯部的要求是：胯根要开，就是胯关节要松开。《拳论》讲："腰如车轴，气如车轮。"腰部的左右旋转和腿部的虚实转换，是靠胯关节的松活来完成的。如果两个胯关节不松活，死顶住骨盆，腰也难以起到车轴的作用。"松胯"这一要求一般是不太好掌握的，因为胯部支撑着上半身的重量。胯部放松，膝关节的负担就要加重。一般初练的人，腿部力量差，膝关节支持不了全身的重量，所以不敢松胯，形成膝盖前栽、鼓肚挺胸、身体后仰的不良姿势。正确的要求是：保持躯干部的中正安舒，下蹲时，膝盖不能超过前脚尖，胯部和臀部像是后边有凳子坐着一样。膝关节的放松，又必须与肩关节的放松上下结合。如果胯不松而肩硬向下垂，肋部和腹部肌肉受压，影响肋部、腹部肌肉的松弛下沉及膈肌的下降，升降功能就会不同程度地受到影响，就难以达到"腹内松静气腾然"的要求。

Chen Family Taijiquan's requirement on hip is root of hip should open, that is, hip joint should open. *Quan Lun* says that waist is like axle and breath (*qi*) is like wheel. Revolving of waist and transition of legs is accomplished by opening and closing of hip joint. If hip joint can not open and close and always stand up to pelivis, waist is difficult to play the role of axle. "Open hip" is difficult to master because hip supports the weight of upper body. When hips relax, burden of hip joint will be increased. Generally, power on new practioner's leg is weak and hip joint can not support the weight of whole body, so he dares not to open his hip, which is easy to form the style as knees lean forward, bringing convex and bending backward. The correct style is keeping body upright; the knees can't overtop tiptoe when squatting down, as if you seat on a stool with buttocks. The relaxation of knees joint must be combined with relaxation of shoulder joint. If hip can't loose and shoulder drooping, then oppress the muscle of belly and flank, it will cause the muscle of belly and flank sink and muscular diaphragm droop. Fluctuation function will be influenced as different degree. So it can't satisfy the requirement that abdomen is empty and loose so breath (*qi*) can rise naturally.

3. 膝 Knees

膝是由关节和关节韧带等周围组织所组成。活动性能好，伸缩力强，是胫腓骨与股骨的结合部。它在太极拳运动中的地位也是非常重要的，因为太极拳是在曲膝松胯的基础上保持立身中正。在整套架式练习时，膝关节始终保持一定的弯曲。拳架身法的高低，步法的大小，都与膝关节有直接的关系。从身法上讲，身法低，步定人，膝节关承受负担就重。在套路练习中，腿部支撑力的大小、全身的重量，都是由膝关节的调节来完成的。

初学太极拳的人，应该先练高身法，待腿上有了支撑力，再逐渐降低身法。这样由高到低，活动量由小到大，循序渐进，以免膝关节受伤。同时还要注意膝关节的保护。练拳之后，关节及身体组织血液运行加速，关节局部有热感。这时，皮窍开而腠理松，千万不可用冷水洗或风吹，以免风湿乘机入侵，引起关节皮肉的风湿痹症。

陈氏太极拳在技击上对膝部也有一定的要求，双人推手，两腿相并，两膝互相粘化，可以外撇、里扣、膝打，既可迫使对方失势，也是护裆、护耻骨的方法。拳论有"远用足踢，近便加膝"的说法。

Knees are consisted of joints and the tissue around ligament joint. They have the good function of activity and strong flexibility, they are combining site of tibia and thighbone. The posture in Taijiquan is also important. Because Taijiquan should keep body upright on the basic of bending knees and relaxing hip, so the joint of knees must keep bending when you exercise the whole posture. The height of fist and the size of the stepping are all closely related to with knees joint. For the action, lower body and slower stepping will cause more burdens to knees joint. The size of support power of leg and the all body's weight are adjusted by knees joint in the exercise.

Beginner of Taijiquan should exercise high posture and then reduce the posture after he has enough power on leg to support himself. Practicing from the easy to the hard and from the small to the large can prevent knees to being hurt. At the same time, pay attention to protecting your knees joint. After exercising, the circulation of blood in joint and body speed up, and some positions of joint became heated. At this time, skin open its pores and tissues, so don't wash with cold water or blow by wind to prevent rheumatism enter body, resulting in rheumatism.

As to the view of practicing skill, Chen Family Taijiquan has requirement on knees. When two persons push hands with each other, their legs are parallel together with knees close together. Their legs can extend outward, withdrew inward and attack with knees. This can force the opponent to lose his strength and simultaneously protect his own crotch and pubis. *Quan Lun* says, "To tick with foot when far and to attack with knee when near."

4. 足 Foot

足是周身之根基。两足姿势的正确，对保证步法的灵活稳健有重要的作用。陈氏太极拳对两足的要求是：两足踏实地，足趾、足掌、足后跟皆要抓地，涌泉穴（正脚心）要虚。足趾不能跷，足掌不能左撇右歪、前搓后晃。在开步及迈步时，要定准方向和位置，要做到"落地生根"，不能乱动。这样，才有步履清晰、沉着、稳健的感觉。

另外，在运行中，向前迈步或向左右开步时，都要曲膝松胯，足尖上翘里合，足跟里侧着地，向外铲地滑出，开到适当的位置，再移重心落实。向后退时，足尖先落地，再移重心逐渐踏实。在向左右方向旋转时，一足支撑重心，另一足足尖上跷外摆或里扣，以足跟外侧着地，方向位置移好，再移重心踏实。足尖外摆和里扣时，要使腿部具有螺旋缠丝劲。

足在技击上可分为钩、套、蹬、踢、踩等方法。钩、套、踢一般是用足尖的方法；蹬、踩是用足跟及足掌的方法。

以上对周身各部位的要求，贯穿于整个太极拳套路中，它们是相互依存、相互联系、相互制约的。任何一部分的姿势正确与否，都会影响全身。局部可影响全身，全身可影响局部。所以初学的人，必须细心揣摩，认真思考，按照全身各部位的要求，在基本功上打好基础，这样才能逐渐在整个套路运行中，将各部位的姿势恰当地配合，从而掌握动作中的速度、路线和方法，逐渐达到身端步稳、动作连贯圆活、节节贯串、上下相随、周身协调、一动全动、一气呵成、动如流水静若山、慢如行云疾似电的高级境界。

注：人的椎骨未成年时为三十四（或三十三）块，成年人的五块骶椎合成为一块骶骨，五（或四）块尾椎合成为一块尾骨。

Foot is the foundation of whole body. Posture of feet is very important to ensure stepping agile and stable. Chen Family Taijiquan's requirement on foot is to stand on ground firmly with toes, sole and heel grasp ground and with *Yongquan* Acupoint (which is located in the center of foot) empty. Toes should not cock up and sole can not incline to right or left. When stepping and striding, position its direction and location so as to achieve "stepping roots on the ground". Thus, the stepping will be clear, stable and calm.

When practicing, striding forward or both sides should keep knee bended and hip relaxed, with toes raising up inward and with heel's inner side landing and shoveling and sliding outward. When stepping on to its right position, move body's center of gravity and step firmly and solidly. When revolving from right to left, one foot supports body's center of gravity. The other toe raises up and swings outward or hooks inside and outside of the heel. When position is fixed, move center of gravity again. When toe raises up outward or hooks inside, the leg should have screwing wrapping energy.

In the factor of practicing skill, foot can be divided into hook, sheathe, mount, kick and tread. Hook, sheathe and kick is finished by toe and mount and tread by the heel and the sole.

All the above requirements on each part of body should be satisfied in Taijiquan practice. They depend on each other, have close relationship with each other and also are restrict to each other. Whether the posture of each part is right or not it will bring influence to the whole body. Locality will influence the whole body and the whole body also can bring influence to each part of body. Beginner should study carefully and make a good start from basic skill according to Taijiquan's requirement on every part of body. So he can keep posture of each part coordinated well when practicing and mastering the speed, stepping and method. As time goes on, he can slowly achieve a supper state in which his practicing is easy and fluent, like flowing water when moving and a mountain when keeping still, like floating cloud when slowing down and flash when speeding up so as to keep body healthy, stable and agile.

Note: There are 34 or 33 backbones when people are in their teenagers and 5 hip bones will combined into one and 5 or 4 coccygeal bones will become into one coccyx.

第五节
陈氏太极拳的独特方法
UNIQUENESS OF CHEN-STYLE TAIJIQUAN

一、把拳术与引导、吐纳术相结合
Combining Boxing Techniques with Daoyin and Tuna Practice

引导和吐纳术是中华民族很古老的养身术，汉末伟大的医学家华佗创编的"五禽戏"，是模仿禽兽屈伸顾盼、跳跃等动作，并结合呼吸运动来健身，也就是后来的气功和内行功的演变。

陈王廷把武术中的手眼身法学的协调动作，同导引、吐纳结合起来，使意识、呼吸和动作三者密切配合成为"内外合一"的内家拳功。

Daoyin (channeling and leading internal energy) and *Tuna* (deep breathing exercises) are traditional health enhancing methods for Chinese people. "Five Animals Exercise" created by the famous doctor Hua Tuo in the late Han dynasty, imitates animals' movements including bending, stretching, gazing, jumping and so on, and combined with breathing for body building, which later evolved into *Qigong* and *Neixinggong*. Chen Wangting, by combining the harmonious movements of hands, eyes and body with *Daoyin* and *Tuna* practice, created the united boxing of internal and external integrity through the close cooperation of consciousness, breath and movement.

二、把武术和中医经络学相结合
Combining Wushu with Chinese Medicine Theories of Jingluo

经络是指布满人体的气血通路，源于脏腑，流于肢体。脏腑经络，气血失调，则神肌反常而疾病生。通则气血流畅，强身延年。陈王廷根据自己的心得体会，结合经络学说的道理，创编成缠绕螺旋运动方式的陈氏太极拳械套路。

Jingluo means meridian circulation channels along which the acupressure points are located. It originates from viscera and flows in the body. If the function of vital energy and the state of blood of viscera meridian lose balance, the appearance and body will be abnormal and illness comes. While if the meridian channels are free, the energy and blood will flow freely which is good for health and life span. According to his own understanding and theories of meridian, Chen Wangting created Chen-style Taijiquan and weapon forms based on spiral reeling movement.

三、创编了双人推手技法
Creating Partner Push-hands Technique

自古以来，跌、打、摔、拿、跃是我国武术的五大主要技击法，由于这五种技击法在实践中有较大的伤害性，历来都只做假想性或象征性的练习。这就为花假手法开了方便之门，而前人苦心积累的宝贵经验，也由于时间不足，很难提高技击水平。鉴于此，陈王廷才创造了推手方法，这种方法伤害性较轻，成为一种综合性的实习技击的练习方法。

From early times, the main combat techniques of Wushu have been throwing, hitting, falling, grabbing and jumping. As the above techniques have great possibility of injury in practice, generally the exercise can only be pretending or symbolic, which leads to the showy postures. Meanwhile, lack of time makes it difficult to learn the valuable experience and improve combat level. Therefore, Chen Wangting created push-hands technique and its low injury possibility means it can be one comprehensive exercise method for practical combat.

四、创编了双人刺枪和杆梢对练方法
Creating partner spear-thrusting and Long-pole pair practice

陈王廷创编了双人粘枪法，粘随不脱、蓄发相变的刺枪和杆梢对练，是陈氏太极拳器械的对抗性基本练习方法，结合陈氏拳术里面与众不同的螺旋缠丝劲，运用在拳械之上，为拳械对练开辟了一条简便易行、提高技艺的途径。

Chen Wangting created partner spear-thrusting method without separating through adhering and following. Partner practices of spear-thrusting and long-pole are the basic practice methods for the confrontation of Taiji weapons. The application of its unique silk reeling energy to the weapon practice shows an easy way to improve techniques of partner weapon practice.

五、对陈氏太极拳的理论认定
Theoretical Acknowledge of Chen-style Taijiquan

陈氏太极拳理论是陈王廷根据自己的实践经验，总结和吸取了明代民间武术经验与各种拳术理论写成的。陈氏太极拳理论是缠绕螺旋、柔中寓刚、避实击虚、顺应客观条件而变化、以意形气、劲由内换、人不知我、我独知人、因敌变化的理论体系。《拳经总歌》开篇说："纵放屈伸人莫知，诸靠缠绕我皆依。"从而在练习陈氏太极拳套路的基础上练习反应灵敏，逐步达到"牵动四两拨千斤"的高级境界。

自陈王廷之后，陈家沟习武风甚盛，老幼妇孺均练习，因此当地流传着谚语："喝了陈家沟的水，都会蹺蹺腿"，"人人都会金刚大捣碓。"这种习武之风世代沿袭，经久不衰，历代高手辈出。

The heories on Chen-style Taijiquan by Chen Wangting is based on his own experience and knowledge about folk experience on Wushu in Ming dynasty and various boxing theories. It is the theoretical system which includes silk reeling of internal spiral energy hardness implied in softness avoiding the substantial to attack the substantial change with objective conditions, breath (*qi*) formed from intention

(*Yi*), internal change of energy the opponent not knowing me while I knowing the opponent and change by the opponent. The first two sentences in A *General Formula of Boxing Treatises* say "the movements bending or stretching the opponent knows not push-hands and silk reeling I depend". So practice quick responses on the basis of Chen-style Taijiquan forms exercise and gradually reaches the advance level of "four ounces redirecting thousand pounds".

After Chen Wangting's times, martial arts practice in Chenjiagou Village began to prevail. Therefore, one saying goes there, "If you drink the water in Chenjiagou, you can raise your legs (learn some movements of Taiji)." Another saying is "Everyone knows Jingang Hammer". The custom of martial arts practice has passed down from generation to generation with the birth of grandmasters.

第六节
陈氏太极拳的技击作用
COMBAT FUNCTION OF CHEN-STYLE TAIJIQUAN

中华武术，门派繁多，攻防技巧，各有所长，拳打脚踢，谓之一般。然而，陈氏太极拳却独树一帜，不仅能起到健身作用，而且在技击方面也奥妙无穷。流传了三百余年，仍保持其本色。它以掤、捋、挤、按、采、挒、肘、靠为中心内容，在粘、连、相、随的基础上，将抓、拿、摔、滑、打、跌熔为一炉，内外兼练，成为我国武坛上最优秀的拳种之一。

练习陈氏太极拳，三年一小成，九年一大成，练到上乘功夫，可达周身一家，以静制动，以逸待劳，以不变而应万变，亦可得机得势，舍己从人，随机应变，灵活运用，引进落空，借力打人。有推手歌云："掤捋挤须认真，周身相随人难侵，任人巨力来打我，牵动四两拨千斤。"

推手，不仅可以检验姿势是否正确，也是锻炼技击技巧的好方法。有人说："推手有何技巧，力大者即可取胜。"《太极拳论》中说："斯技旁门甚多，虽有区别，概不外乎壮欺弱，慢让快耳。有力打无力，手慢让手快，是皆先天自然之能，非关学力而有为也。察四两拨千斤之句，显非力胜，观老老能御众之形，快何能为？"可见，太极拳之推手不是比力而是比技巧。"壮欺弱、慢让快"那是自然的本能，不是技巧的功能。所谓技巧，则是顺应自然以利用自然，达到"弱胜壮、慢胜快"。自然界中的杠杆支点和螺旋转化的原理，就具有"四两拨千斤"的功能。推手利用这种原理，就具有"四两拨千斤"的功能。推手利用这种原理，即可柔化一切重力，为化劲。有此化劲功夫，就可以轻制重。同时，太极拳的运动是运用了离心力与向心力，并以腰脊作中轴，使一切动作皆走内圈；走内圈虽速度较慢，但仍可胜过走外圈的；这是"后人发，先人至"的缘由，也是"慢胜快"的关键所在。

For various schools of Chinese Wushu, attack and defiance skills are different while hitting by hand and kicking by feet are all the same.

However, Chen-style Taijiquan shows its uniqueness in combined functions of body building and martial application. With a history of over 300 years, it keeps the original characteristics of its focus on Ward Off (*peng*), Roll Back (*lu*), Press (*ji*), Push (*an*), Pull Down (*cai*), Rend (*lie*), Elbow Stroke (*zhou*), Shoulder Stroke (*kao*) and its integrity of grabbing, seizing, throwing, dodging, beating, falling, on the basis of adhere, contact, stick and follow. Now by internal and external exercise it has been one of the best boxing in Chinese Wushu field.

For practice of Chen-style Taijiquan three years means some progress, nine years means great achievement. When practice comes to the top stage it can be attained that the entire body works as a whole, stillness counteracts movement, ease waits for exhaustion, the constant is used. For the flexible and meanwhile the practitioner can get opportunity, follow the opponent, make changes wisely direct opponent to the emptiness and make use of the opponents force for attack. In one Push-hands song are the following words: "In War-off, Rollback, Press and Push, you must be very conscientious. Up and down follow one another, make it difficult for your opponent to enter. Let him attack me with great force, and I use my four ounces to redirect his thousand pounds."

Push-hands can be used to check if the posture is correct. And also used to practice combat skills. Some people say, "No skill is necessary for push-hands; the one with great force can win."

In the book *Taijiquan Treatise*, it says, "There are many other kinds of martial arts, although their forms are distinct from one another, overall they are nothing more than the strong taking advantage of the weak, or merely the slow yielding to the quick. Having strength to strike those without strength, the slow of hand giving way to the quick of hand. These are all from inherent natural ability and bear no relationship to the capability that comes from earnest study. Examine the expression four ounces deflect one thousand pounds." Clearly this is not accomplished by means of strength. Observe a situation in which one who is aged can skillfully fend off a young.

How can this ability be one of speed? So it can be seen that push-hands in

Taijiquan is not the competition in force, but in skill. It is the natural ability but not the function of skills that the strong beats the weak, the slow yields to the fast. Skill means compliance with nature for making use of nature to reach the goal that the weak can beat the strong and the slow can defeat the fast. In nature, the fulcrum of lever and spiral conversion show the function of "four ounces redirecting thousand pounds", which is applied to push-hand to mix and redirect the heavy forces so that the light can control the heavy. Meanwhile Taijiquan by means of centrifugal and centripetal force with lumbar spine as the central axis makes all movements go around the internal circle which despite the low linear speed can overtake the fast movements around the external circles. This can account for "late starting but early arriving", and is also the key part for the slow to win the fast.

练习推手应遵守以下四项基本原则：

1.《太极拳论》中说："太极者，无极而生，动静之机，阴阳之母也，动之则分，静之则合。"古时所称"太极"，是对立统一的象征，是一切动静的枢机。由太极生阴阳，如顺逆、柔刚、轻沉、虚实、合开等皆属于此。运动时充分利用了离心力和向心力，因此动之则分，静之则合，分为阳，合为阴。《拳经》中说："太极两仪，天地阴阳，合辟动静，柔之为刚"，就是指这种规律。这种矛盾存在于推手的整个过程中，并贯穿于每一个动作过程的始终。因此，推手的第一个基本原则，就是它要符合事物运动的矛盾法则，即"矛盾与开合"。

Push-hands practice shall follow the four basic principles below.

Firstly, in the book *Taijiquan Treatise* the supreme ultimate born out of no extremity is the chance of movement and stillness, mother of *Yin* and *Yang*, movement means dividing and stillness, means reuniting. The ancient "supreme ultimate" is the symbol of the unity of opposites, the vital element of movement and stillness and originate of *Yin* and *Yang* including submit and resist, soft and hard, light and heavy, reality and emptiness, reunite and divide, etc. In movement, it makes full use of centrifugal and centripetal forces. So movement means dividing, which is *Yang* and stillness means reuniting which is *Yin*. This classic law that is explained in the supreme ultimate has double forms of the heaven and the earth as *Yin* and *Yang*, close and open as stillness and movement, softness as hardness. The contradiction appears in the whole push-hands process and also the complete process of each movement. Therefore, the first principle for push-hands is to follow the law of contradiction in the movement, i. e. contradiction and open/close.

2. 推手时双方搭手对练的过程，也是不断产生矛盾和解决矛盾的过程。《太极拳论》中所说"无过不及，随屈就伸"，就是指动作必须符合下列四点：

（1）必须"无过"：无过称为"粘劲"，过则称为"顶病"；

（2）必须"能及"：能及称为"相劲"，过则称为"匾病"；

（3）必须"随曲"：随曲称为"连劲"，不随而曲称为"丢病"；

（4）必须"就伸"：就伸称为"随劲"，伸得太早称为"抗病"。

推手的一切过程都要求具有"粘、连、相、随"等方法，不发生"顶、匾、丢、抗"四病。《拳经》中说："粘连相随，会神聚精，运我虚灵，弥加整重。"所以，第二个基本原则是"粘连相随"。

Secondly, the process of push-hands is that of producing and solving contradiction. In the book *Taijiquan Treatise*, it says "neither excess nor deficiency, follow the opponent to compress or extend", which means the movement must meet the requirements below:

1. No excess, which is called "stick power", while excess is called "Ding Fault".

2. Reachable, which is called "adhere power", while excess is called "Bian Fault".

3. Follow to compress, which is called "connect power ", or, it is called "Losing Fault".

4. Follow to extend, which is called "follow power", or, extending early is called "Resisting Fault".

All the processes of push-hands shall inclued the methods of adhere, connect, stick and follow, and avoid the faults of going against equilibrium, deficiency, losing and resisting.

Quan Jing says adhere, connect, stick and follow to concentrate the mind, use the emptiness so as to embody the whole and the heavy. Therefore the second principle is adhere, connect, stick and follow.

3.《太极拳论》中说："人刚我柔谓之走，我顺人背谓之粘；动急则急应，动缓则缓随；虽变化万端，而理为一贯。"这是为了能做到随变化而变化，避免四病的措施。这就是说，人刚则我柔，用"走"以引之。这是被动局面下的"捲合"运用。同时，为了问劲，运用顺遂的势和劲，迫使对方成为"背"，转化为我刚人柔，用粘以逼之。粘走时，对方动急则急应之，动缓则缓随之，这样就可有变化而无四病。《拳论》说："前后左右，上下四旁，转接灵敏，缓急相将。"所以，第三个基本原则是"急缓粘走"。

Thirdly, in the book *Taijiquan Treatise*, it says, "When the other is hard, and I am soft, this is called yielding. I go along with the other. This is called adhering. To quick movements, I respond quickly. To slow movements, I follow slowly. Although the transformations have innumerable strands, this principle makes them as one thread." This is used to change and also to avoid the four faults. That is, when the opponent is hard, I become soft to direct the opponent by this yielding, which is application of rolling up and reuniting in the passive situation. At the same time, through following the posture and power, the opponent is forced. To be not in his favor and I become hard to approach by adhering. While adhering, to the opponent's fast move, I follow fast; to his slow movement, I follow slowly. In this way, change is achieved without the four faults. Quan Lun says, "For back and forth, right and left, up and down, turn and contact shall be quick and change is needed for being fast or slowly". Therefore, the third basic principle is "fast and slowly adhering and yielding".

4.《太极拳论》中说："由着熟而渐悟懂劲，由懂劲而阶及神明，然非用功之久，不能豁然贯通焉。"在推手时熟练地掌握了前面三个基本原则后，就可领悟人劲，探测对方的劲力与方向，是谓懂得人劲。到此时，可信手而应，达到自动的"神明"境界。这是多年反复揣摩、实践和理论研究，最后得到豁然贯通的结果。所以，第四个基本原则是"实践和理论相一致"。

《太极拳论》中说："虚领顶劲，气沉丹田；不偏不倚，忽隐忽显，左重则左虚，右重则右杳；仰之则弥高，俯之则弥深；进之则愈长，退之则愈促；一羽不能加，蝇虫不能落；人不知我，我独知人；英雄所向无敌，盖皆由此而及也。"因此，为了运用以上四项基本原则，就必须按照上列拳论做好以下六点：

（1）顶劲要虚虚领起，则精神自然提起，同时气沉丹田，周身放松。由于身体上领下沉，致使身躯放长而产生弹性，成为掤劲。《拳经》中说："沿路缠缠，静远无慌，肌肤骨节，处处开张。"若是周身僵力，就会失去掤劲，也就不能通过粘、相、连、随去求懂劲。

（2）立身顺中正安舒，具有支撑八面之势，推手时，身躯不致偏于一边或依赖于对方身手之上，以免己劲为人所识。若偏一边，就不易顺遂地运用"粘走"功夫。

（3）在神气内陷则柔、外显则刚的前提下，推手时要具有忽隐忽显的刚柔变换作用，这正是求懂劲过程中不断问劲的表现。

（4）推手时，要求做到两手有虚实，两足有虚实，一手一足上下亦要分虚实，形成处处分阴阳，处处有虚实。《拳经》中说："虚实兼到，忽见忽藏；实中有虚，人己相参；虚中有实，熟测机关。"待虚实的转换熟练后，只要注意一只手，其他一只手、两只足由于上下相随，自然也就能随着灵换。所以《拳经》中又说："千古一日，至理循环，上下相随，不可空谈。"这是问劲、化劲和达到懂劲的基础。

（5）对方仰来，则高以引之，使有高不可攀之感而失去重心；对方俯来，则愈向下引，使有如临深渊、摇摇欲坠之感；对方近迫，则愈引、愈虚，使有长不可及之感；对方退走，则粘逼，使有迫促之感；这是符合粘、连、相、随的化劲与发劲要求的，这样就可避免发生顶、匾、丢、抗四病，使推手技巧迅速提高。

（6）推手时，精神须提起，这样周身才能轻灵贯串，并要轻灵得具有"羽不能加"的敏感。同时螺旋缠丝也须不断变动，要旋转得形成"蝇虫不能落"之气势。若动作表现出迟重不灵，则不易懂劲；若运动没有缠丝，则失去化劲，也失去半化半进、明化暗进、即化即进的缠丝劲技巧。没有化劲，就变成比力，就不为太极拳推手了。能化而不能发、能柔而动刚、刚柔不能相济，都非太极两仪之全。

具有上列六项功能，就能贯彻推手的四项基本原则，达到懂得人劲而不为人懂的功夫，再加上乾乾之功，便可使推手技巧达到炉火纯青的高级境界。

Fourthly, the book *Taijiquan Treatise* says, "The practiced gradually understand the energy from which comes the deity, but the enlightenment cannot be obtained without time-consuming practice." After mastering the above three principles for push-hands, one can understand human energy and explore the energy power and direction of the opponent, which is knowing energy. Up to now, one can respond freely and reach the level of deity. It is the state of enlightenment from years repeated thinking, practice and theoretical research. Therefore, the fourth basic principle is compliance of practice with theory.

The book *Taijiquan Treatise* says, "An intangible and lively energy lifts the crown of the head, the *qi* sinks to the *Dantian*, no leaning, no inclining, suddenly hidden, suddenly appearing. When the left feels weight, then the left empties. When the right feels weight, then the right is gone. Looking up, it then becomes yet higher. Looking down, it then becomes yet deeper. Advancing, there is an even longer distance. Retreating, it is then even more crowded. One feather cannot be added. A fly cannot land. The other does not know me; I alone know the other. This is to be a hero with no adversaries along the way. Does it not all come from this?" So to apply the above four basic principles, the following six points are important.

1. When the crown of the head is suspended from above, the spirit is naturally raised and at the same time, breath sinks to the *Dantian*, and the entire body is relaxed. Because the above is suspended and the below sinks, ward-off energy is produced by the elastic body from lengthening. Boxing classics says, "When the body is extending in the relaxed state, all the muscles, skins bones and joints will be open." If the entire body is stiff, it will lose ward-off energy, and will not know energy by adhere, connect stick and follow.

2. Standing body shall be centered, straight, stable and comfortable, which shows its support for all the sides, and avoids leaning to one side, or depending on the opponent during push-hands process, in which the energy will be seen by the opponent. If the body leans to one side, it is not easy to make use of adhering and yielding.

3. As the premise that inward hiding is softness and outward display is hardness, push-hands shall have the function of change between softness and hardness with hiding and display. This is the demonstration of inquiring energy attempts during seeking for energy knowledge.

4. For push-hands, it is required that the hands shall have reality and emptiness, and the same as the feet. And the hand above and the foot below shall also have reality and emptiness forms everywhere there is *Yin* and *Yang*, reality and emptiness forms. Boxing classics says, "Combine reality and emptiness which is suddenly seen and suddenly hidden, including emptiness in reality to mix one and the opponent, and realty in emptiness to get good estimate of chances." After the fractionalized has a good command of changes between reality and emptiness, it is necessary to focus on one hand, the other hand and the feet will follow and change accordingly. Therefore, boxing classics also says, "One day for the sands of time has its cycle and it is not empty talk for following of the above and below." This is the basis for inquiring, resolving and then understanding energy.

5. When the incoming force is upward, I follow and become higher to let the opponent feel too high to reach and lose his center of gravity. When the incoming force is downward, I still follow and become deeper to let the opponent feel at

the edge of abyss to fall easily. Direct further and have more emptiness when the opponent approaches nearer to let him feel the increasing distance while adhere to approach when he retreats to let him feel the urgent chasing. It meets the requirements of resolving and originating energy in adhere-connect and stick-follow, in which way the faults can be avoided and push-hand skills can be improve quickly.

6. For push-hands, the spirit shall be raised so that the entire body can work as a whole and become so light and alert that even a feather cannot be added. Meanwhile, silk reeling-internal spiral energy shall turn to reach the state that a fly cannot land. If the movement is not quick, it is not easy to know energy, whereas if there is no silk reeling for the movement, it means the loss of transforming energy and skills of the silk-reeling energy—half transforming with half advancing, display transforming with hidden advancing, and advancing while transforming. In case of no energy transformation it is the competition in forces but not Taijiquan push-hands. It will not show the double when advancing fails in transforming; hardness is used while softness can do and softness and hardness cannot couple with each other.

After the above six functions can be attained, the practioner can follow the four basic principles for push-hands, and reach the state of knowing energy of the opponent but not being known. Then with the energy from the universe, one can reach the acme of perfection in push-hand skills.

第七节
陈氏太极拳的螺旋缠丝劲
THE SILK REELING-INTERNAL SPIRAL
ENERGY OF CHEN-STYLE TAIJIQUAN

　　陈氏太极拳的螺旋缠丝劲就是旋转地运动身体的每一个地方。平时运动时能掌握此劲道者，与对方交手时，自然此劲道就会行到身体的每一个地方，想完全掌握螺旋缠丝劲，必须长时间正确地练习。其劲道包括顺缠逆缠、进缠退缠、上缠下缠、里缠外缠、左缠右缠、前缠后缠和大缠小缠。想要缠好此劲，还须分清此劲道要围绕在以丹田为核心的缠绕运动，任何的动作皆是阴阳互变之理。如果身体过于软而无力，怎能应变而变化？但是表面不能过于僵硬，所以表面形柔，里面形刚，身体全部部位之作用，头劲要上领，劲要撑圆，并且要相合转换，两肩两肘要松沉，配合手眼，眼要平视前方，手为先锋在前，头顶不可歪，心要平静如水，两膝开合转换有方，胸腰含塌要协调一致，两足要踏实，两腿劲力虚实要清。其表面之形态安然自如，外形秀若处子，不能表现出浮躁之气、狂妄自大，要尽显大家风范。交手之中，其必要静，物来顺应，自然退、攻、防、重自控，此中太极之阴阳变化，无须偏倚，此乃开合之妙用，螺旋缠丝劲自明也。

　　Chen-style Taijiquan silk reeling energy is to move each part of the body around the spiral bone. In combating, the one who has mastered that energy method will naturally move the energy to each part of the body. To have a good command of silk reeling of internal spiral energy, long-time proper practice is necessary. Taijiquan is equivalent to the method of winding silk. The method of winding silk can be divided into winding smooth and adverse, advancing and retreating, winding left and right, winding up and down, winding inside and outside, winding large and small, winding directly and indirectly, and so on. For successful high and low reeling energy, it is necessary to know the reeling is centered on *Dantian* any movement demonstrates the law of change between *Yin* and *Yang*, if the body is too soft and weak, how can it react to changes? However, the outside shall not be too stiff, so the outside is soft while the inside is hard. For the functions of all parts, the energy of head is suspended from above to the degree of the burst of energy and can also reunite and transform; the shoulders and elbows hang freely with hands and eyes. Eyes look straight forward; hands are in front as pioneers; the crown of head cannot be slanting; heart is calm; kneels open and close by certain rules; the maintaining and concaving of chest and waist go together; feet are steadfast; the reality and emptiness of the legs' energy shall be clear. The appearance shows the peacefulness and elegance like a maid, and manifests the air of a master without impetuosity or arrogance. During confronting, stillness is in need; yield for the coming object and it will retreat naturally, and control the attack and defense the change of *Yin* and *Yang* with no leaning in it is the wise application of dividing and reuniting, and silk reeling energy can be self-evident now.

第八节
陈氏太极拳历代人物介绍
THE IMPORTANT CHARACTERS OF CHEN-STYLE TAIJIQUAN FOR AGES

陈卜（陈氏始祖） Chen Bu (Ancestor of Chen Clan)

陈卜，陈家沟陈氏始祖。

陈卜自小精通拳械，武艺高强，经常替百姓打抱不平，威名远扬。邻村百姓纷纷带孩子来拜师求艺，于是，陈卜便在村中办了一个武学社，授徒传艺，至此，陈家世代习武沿袭至今。

Chen Bu is one ancestor of Chen Clan in Chenjiagou.

Chen Bu was skillful in boxing weapons when he was young and had a high level of martial arts. He won his fame because he always defended people against the injustice. As many parents from neighborhood brought their children to learn from him, Chen Bu set up a martial arts society in the village to teach students there. Hence practice of martial arts in each generation of Chen clan till now.

陈王廷（九世高祖） Chen Wangting (The 9th Generation Ancestor)

陈王廷，字奏庭，系陈家沟陈氏第九世太极拳的创始人。

陈王廷文武兼备，依据祖传拳械，博采诸家拳法之精华，结合中医经络学和导引吐纳术，以中华传统阴阳学说为理论依据，创编了武术、传统文化、医学三者相融合的流传至今的"陈氏太极拳"。

Chen Wangting, styled Zouting and is the creator of the 9th generation Chen Family Taijiquan. Chen Wangting, who adopts with both pen and sword, has created "Chen Family Taijiquan" with the integrity of Wushu, traditional culture and medicine on the bases of ancestral boxing and weapons, the essence of various boxing forms, combination with traditional Chinese meridian and Taoist breathing exercise method, and Chinese traditional negative (*Yin*) and positive (*Yang*) theory.

陈汝信（十世高祖） Chen Ruxin (The 10th Generation Ancestor)

陈汝信，陈家沟陈氏第十世高祖，陈氏太极拳嫡系传人，为太极拳的延续起到承上启下的重要作用。

Chen Ruxin is the 10th generation lineage holder of Chen Family Taijiquan in Chenjiagou and play the linking role in continuity of Taijiquan.

陈大鹏（十一世高祖） Chen Dapeng (The 11th Generation Ancestor)

陈大鹏，陈家沟陈氏第十一世高祖，陈氏太极拳嫡系传人。在传承家学方面为后人做出巨大贡献。

Chen Dapeng is the 11th generation lineage holder of Chen Family Taijiquan in Chenjiagou, who has contributed much to carrying on Chen Family Taijiquan.

陈大鹍（十一世高祖） Chen Dakun (The 11th Generation Ancestor)

陈大鹍，陈家沟陈氏第十一世高祖，陈氏太极拳嫡系传人。

Chen Dakun is the 11th generation lineage holder of Chen Family Taijiquan in Chenjiagou.

陈善志（十二世高祖） Chen Shanzhi (The 12th Generation Ancestor)

陈善志，陈家沟陈氏第十二世高祖，陈氏太极拳嫡系传人。

Chen Shanzhi is the 12th generation lineage holder of Chen Family Taijiquan in Chenjiagou.

陈善通 （十二世高祖）　Chen Shantong (The 12th Generation Ancestor)

陈善通，陈家沟陈氏第十二世高祖，陈氏太极拳嫡系传人。

Chen Shantong is the 12th generation lineage holder of Chen Family Taijiquan in Chenjiagou.

陈秉壬（十三世高祖）　Chen Bingren (The 13th Generation Ancestor)

陈秉壬，陈家沟陈氏第十三世高祖，陈氏太极拳嫡系传人。

Chen Bingren is the 13th generation lineage holder of Chen Family Taijiquan in Chenjiagou.

陈秉奇（十三世高祖）　Chen Bingqi (The 13th Generation Ancestor)

陈秉奇，陈家沟陈氏第十三世高祖，陈氏太极拳嫡系传人。

Chen Bingqi is the 13th generation lineage holder of Chen Family Taijiquan in Chenjiagou.

陈秉旺（十三世高祖）　Chen Bingwang (The 13th Generation Ancestor)

陈秉旺，陈家沟陈氏第十三世高祖，陈氏太极拳嫡系传人。

Chen Bingwang is the 13th generation lineage holder of Chen Family Taijiquan in Chenjiagou.

陈长兴（十四世高祖）　Chen Changxing (The 14th Generation Ancestor)

陈长兴，字云亭，陈家沟陈氏第十四世高祖，陈氏太极拳嫡系传人。

陈长兴在发展、弘扬、传承陈氏太极拳方面，将祖传的太极拳由博归约、去芜存菁，归纳整理出一套更加体现太极拳原理的老架一、二两个套路。又将太极拳理和武术思想相结合，整理出了一套完整的武术理论，主要有《太极拳十大要论》、《太极拳用武要言》、《太极拳战斗篇》等著作。

Chen Changxing, styled Yunting, is the 14th generation lineage holder of Chen Family Taijiquan in Chenjiagou. Chen Changxing, while developing and carrying on Chen Family Taijiquan, systematized one set of old Frame (*Laojia*) with two set forms of *Yi Lu* and *Er Lu* which can better embody Taijiquan principles by trimming from broadness to conciseness and by removing superfluous words and retaining essence. Meanwhile, he combined Taijiquan theory with Wushu thought and arranged a complete set of Wushu theory, which mainly consist of the books *Ten Main Theories on Taijiquan*, *Important Words on Martial Application*, *Taijiquan in Fighting*, etc.

陈耕耘（十五世高祖） Chen Gengyun (The 15th Generation Ancestor)

陈耕耘，陈家沟陈氏第十五世高祖，陈氏太极拳嫡系传人。

Chen Gengyun is the 15th generation lineage holder of Chen Family Taijiquan in Chenjiagou.

陈延年（十六世高祖） Chen Yannian (The 16th Generation Ancestor)

陈延年，陈家沟陈氏第十六世高祖，陈氏太极拳嫡系传人。

Chen Yannian is the 16th generation lineage holder of Chen Family Taijiquan in Chenjiagou.

陈延熙（十六世高祖） Chen Yanxi (The 16th Generation Ancestor)

陈延熙，陈家沟陈氏第十六世高祖，陈氏太极拳嫡系传人，对陈氏太极拳的继承和发展做出了不可磨灭的贡献。

Chen Yanxi is the 16th generation lineage holder of Chen Family Taijiquan in Chenjiagou and his efforts in carrying on and developing Chen Family Taijiquan shall be remembered.

陈发科（曾祖） Chen Fake (Great Grandfather)

陈发科（1887—1957），陈家沟陈氏第十七世曾祖，陈氏太极拳嫡系传人，陈氏太极拳新架创始人，对陈氏太极拳的发展、传播做出了杰出贡献，被武林同道尊为"一代宗师"。

陈发科一生授徒甚多，1963年由人民体育出版社出版的《陈氏太极拳》一书，便是由弟子沈家桢、顾留馨所著，其中一、二路太极拳式均根据他晚年拳式所定，是中华民族宝贵的武术遗产。

Chen Fake (1887–1957) is the 17th generation lineage holder of Chen Family Taijiquan in Chenjiagou and creator of New Frame (*Xinjia*) of Chen Family Taijiquan, who has made great contribution to development and spread of Chen Family Taijiquan and is praised by peers in Wushu circle as "grandmaster".

In his life, Chen Fake has many pupils and the book *Chen Family Taijiquan* published by People's Sports Press in 1963 is compiled by his pupils Shen Jiazhen and Gu Liuxin. The *Yi Lu* and *Er Lu* Taijiquan forms in the book are made according to boxing forms in his late years, which has been precious Chinese Wushu legacy.

陈照旭 (余祖) Chen Zhaoxu

陈照旭（1909—1960），陈家沟陈氏第十八世，陈氏太极拳嫡系传人，其一生历尽坎坷曲折，极具传奇色彩，是近代陈氏太极拳的重要代表人物之一。

Chen Zhaoxu (1909–1960) is the 18th generation lineage holder of Chen Family Taijiquan in Chenjiagou and is an important representative of recent Chen Family Taijiquan with rough life experience and legendary.

陈照奎（叔祖） Chen Zhaokui (Granduncle)

陈照奎，生于1928年，系陈家沟陈氏第十八世，陈氏太极拳嫡系传人，精通陈氏太极拳理论及各种套路与擒拿术。其一生对陈氏太极拳的推广、普及和弘扬太极文化做出了巨大贡献。

Chen Zhaokui, born in 1928, is the 18th generation lineage holder of Chen Family Taijiquan in Chenjiagou and an expert in Chen Family Taijiquan theories and various forms and sets and *Qinna* techniques. He has devoted his life to spreading of Chen Family Taijiquan and in popularity and development of Taiji culture.

陈豫侠（姑祖） Chen Yuxia (Grandaunt)

陈豫侠（女），系陈家沟陈氏第十八世，为陈氏太极拳的普及和推广曾做出卓越贡献。

Chen Yuxia, female, the 18th generation descendant of Chen family in Chenjiagou and has made great contribution to the popularity and development of Chen Family Taijiquan.

陈小旺（伯父） Chen Xiaowang (Uncle)

陈家沟太极拳学校校长
陈家沟陈氏第十九世太极拳掌门人
陈小旺世界太极拳总会会长、国际太极拳大师
陈小旺，1945年出生于陈家沟，系陈家沟陈氏第十九世，陈氏太极拳嫡系传人，在承袭世代家传武学的基础上，继承、发展了陈氏太极拳。

President of Chenjiagou Taijiquan School
Authority of the 19th Generation Chen Family Taijiquan of Chenjiagou
Director of Chen Xiaowang World Taijiquan Association and International Taijiquan Master
Chen Xiaowang, born in 1945 in Chenjiagou, is the 19th generation lineage holder of Chen Family Taijiquan in Chenjiagou. He based on the family education of martial arts ,has carried on and developed Chen Family Taijiquan.

陈小星（父亲） Chen Xiaoxing (Father)

陈家沟太极拳学校执行校长
陈家沟陈氏太极拳协会会长

陈小星（兴），1952年出生于陈家沟，陈家沟陈氏第十九世太极拳嫡系传人，陈家沟陈氏第十八世"太极妙手"陈照旭三子，第十七世"太极之尊"陈发科嫡孙，曾荣登美国《功夫》杂志做封面人物。

Executive president of Chenjiagou Taijiquan School

Deputy Director of Wen County Taijiquan Research Association and General Coach.

Chen Xiaoxing, born in 1952 in Chenjiagou, is the 19th generation lineage holder of Chen Family Taijiquan in Chenjiagou. He is the third son of the 18th generation master Chen Zhaoxu who is called "Taiji Magical Figure" and is the grandson of the 17th generation "Taiji Senior" master Chen Fake, and once was the cover hero of *KungFu* magazine in the U.S.

陈瑜（叔父） Chen Yu (Uncle)

陈家沟太极拳学校副校长

陈照奎拳术研究社社长

陈瑜，1962年5月出生于陈家沟，为一代宗师陈照奎之子，陈家沟陈氏第十九世太极拳嫡系传人，被人们称为"雄狮猛虎"，在海内外享有极高的声誉。

Vice president of Chenjiagou Taijiquan School

Director of Chen Zhaokui Chinese Boxing Research Association

ChenYu, born in May of 1962 in Chenjiagou, is the son of grandmaster Chen Zhaokui, and the 19th generation holder of Chen Family Taijiquan in Chenjiagou, who has a high prestige at home and abroad with the nickname "a powerful lion and fierce tiger".

陈自强 Chen Ziqiang

陈家沟太极拳学校副校长兼总教练

陈家沟陈氏太极拳协会秘书长

陈自强，1977年出生于陈家沟陈氏太极拳世家，系陈家沟陈氏太极拳第二十世嫡系传人。他自幼随父亲陈小星

（兴）大师习练家传拳械，并得到二伯父陈小旺的悉心指导，擅长陈氏太极拳套路以及各种器械；对太极推手、散手颇为谙熟，动作弹抖靠发，迅猛冷脆，功夫极具威力。

Vice-president and Chief Coach of the Chenjiagou Training Academy and Chief Secretary of the Chen Family Taijiquan Association in Chenjiagou.

Mr. Chen Ziqiang, was born in the anistocratic Family of Chen Family Taijiquan in Chenjiagou Village in 1977. He is the 20th generation lineage holder of Chen Family Taijiquan in Chenjiagou and has practiced Taijiquan since he was a child under the guidance of his father, Mr. Chen Xiaoxing, and advised by his uncle, Mr. Chen Xiaowang. Through meticulous and dedicated practice of forms of Taijiquan and weapons, he has developed a highly-advanced level of *KungFu* and is skilled in push-hands and self-defense techniques.

作者陈自强（前排中）与父亲陈小星（后排右一）、母亲王玉娥（后排右二）、妹妹陈灵巧（前排右一）、弟弟陈自军（前排右二）合影。

Family Photo: The author Chen Ziqiang (center, front row), the author's father Chen Xiaoxing (back row, the first from the right), the author's mother Wang Yu'er (back row, the second from the right), younger sister Chen Lingqiao (front row, the first from the right), younger brother Chen Zijun (front row, the second from the right)

STEP TEACHING AND DIAGRAM

第一节
陈氏太极拳十九势简介

A BRIEF INTRODUCTION TO THE NINETEEN
POSTURES OF CHEN-STYLE TAIJI QUAN

陈氏太极拳十九势，是陈氏第十九世太极拳掌门人陈小旺大师结合老架、新架、小架于一身所创的陈氏简化太极套路之一。

为了让更多的人了解陈氏太极拳，更好地弘扬陈氏太极拳，陈小旺大师创编了这套陈氏太极拳十九势，此套拳路短小精辟，又不失陈氏太极拳的风格特点。简单易学，是初学者的良师益友。

The nineteen postures of Chen-style Taijiquan, was created by the 19th generation master of Chen-style Taijiquan, Chen xiaowang, who has combined the old set *Laojia*, the new set *Xiaojia* and the small set *Xiaojia,* and then simplified them into this one set.

To make more and more people understand Chen-style Taijiquan, and to carry out Taiji culture, Master Chen created and composed the set of nineteen postures of Taiji movements, which is short and full of essence, but still holds the characteristics of Chen-style Taijiquan. It's easy to learn and suitable for new learners.

第二节
陈氏太极拳十九势动作说明与图解
MOVEMENT EXPLANATIONS OF THE
NINETEEN POSTURES OF CHEN-STYLE TAIJI QUAN

图1

一、起势
Starting Form

1. 立身中心，周身放松，虚领顶劲，双目平视，齿轻叩，唇轻合，面南背北。（图1）

Stand straightly, then relax, uplift emptily, look forward with the line of sight parallel to the ground, close teeth and mouth slightly. Face southward. (Fig 1)

图2

2. 屈膝松胯，含胸塌腰。（图2）

Bend knees and loosen crotches, lower chest and bend waist. (Fig 2)

3. 继续松胯，左胯走后弧，右胯走前弧，重心移至右腿，左脚跟提起，脚尖点地。（图3）

Loosen crotches continuously, go backward curve with left crotch and forward curve with right crotch, transfer the center of body weight to right leg, and lift left heel, with the tiptoe on the ground. (Fig 3)

图3

4. 左脚向左横开一步，前脚掌着地与肩同宽或稍宽于肩。（图4）

Move left foot leftward by a step, with the anterior soles on the ground, with the same width as the shoulders or a little wider than the shoulders. (Fig 4)

5. 左脚跟落地，两脚虚实分明。（图5）

Fall down left heel, with one foot solidly and the other emptily. (Fig 5)

图4

图5

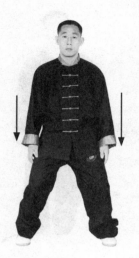

图6

6. 左胯走前弧，右胯走后弧，松左胯，重心移至两腿之间，双目平视，气沉丹田，面南背北。（图6）

Go forward curve with left crotch and backward curve with right crotch, loosen left crotch, transfer the center of body weight between both legs, look forward with the line of sight parallel to the ground and gather *Qi* into *Dantian*. Face southward. (Fig 6)

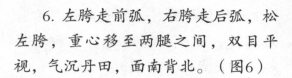

二、金刚出庙
Buddha's Warrior Comes out of the Temple

图7

1. 身法继续下沉，同时双手逆缠上领，与肩同宽同高，掌心向下，松肩沉肘。（图7）

Sink bodily movement continuously, meanwhile twist both hands anticlockwise and uplift, with the same width and level as the shoulders, with the centers of palms downward, and loosen shoulders and sink elbows. (Fig 7)

图8

2. 身法继续下沉，同时双手顺缠下按至体前。（图8）

Sink bodily movement continuously, meanwhile twist both hands clockwise, and press them to the front of body. (Fig 8)

3. 屈膝松胯，左胯走后弧，右胯走前弧，身体稍左转，重心稍右移，同时双手左逆右顺缠，挪至体前。（图9）

Bend knees and loosen crotches, go backward curve with left crotch and forward curve with right crotch, turn body left slightly, transfer the center of body weight rightward slightly, meanwhile twist left hand anticlockwise and right hand clockwise, and prop them to the front of body. (Fig 9)

图9

4. 屈膝松胯，同时，双手左顺右逆缠，坐腕下沉。（图10）

Bend knees and loosen crotches, meanwhile twist it with left hand clockwise and right hand anticlockwise, and sink the base of wrists. (Fig 10)

图10

5. 左胯走前弧，右胯走后弧，重心移至左腿，右脚尖外摆，同时身体右转90°，双手随体转，挪捋至体前，面向西。（图11）

Go forward curve with left crotch and backward curve with right crotch, transfer the center of body weight to left leg, swing right tiptoe outward, meanwhile turn body right by 90°, prop both hands to the front of body along with bodily movement. Face westward. (Fig 11)

图11

6. 屈膝松胯，左胯走后弧，右胯走前弧，身体稍左转，重心右移，目视前方。（图12）

Bend knees and loosen crotches, go backward curve with left crotch and forward curve with right crotch, turn body left slightly, transfer the center of body weight rightward, and look forward. (Fig 12)

图12

7. 左腿屈膝提起，双手外挒。（图13）

Bend left knee to lift, and prop both hands outward. (Fig 13)

图13

8. 左腿向左前45°铲出，脚跟先着地，随即脚掌踏实，屈膝松胯。（图14）

Shovel left forward with left leg by 45°, touch the ground with the heel firstly and then tread solidly with the sole, and bend knees and loosen crotches. (Fig 14)

图14

9. 屈膝松胯，双手左逆，右顺缠，坐腕下沉，气沉丹田。（图15）

Bend knees and loosen crotches, twist left hand anticlockwise and right hand clockwise, sink the base of wrist, and gather *Qi* into *Dantian*. (Fig 15)

图15

10. 左胯走前弧，右胯走后弧，身体左转，左脚尖外摆，重心移至左腿，同时双手左逆，右顺缠走下弧，左手掤至体前掌心向下，右手至右胯外侧，掌心向外，面南背北。（图16）

Go forward curve with left crotch and backward curve with right crotch, turn body left, swing left tiptoe outward, transfer the center of body weight to left leg, meanwhile twist left hand anticlockwise and right hand clockwise to draw downward curve, prop left hand to the front of body, with the palm downward, put right hand to the outside of right crotch, with the palm outward. Face southward. (Fig 16)

图16

11. 右腿向前上步至体前，脚尖点地，双手顺缠合至体前，左手掌心向下合于右小臂内侧，右手掌心向上。（图17）

图17

Step forward with right leg to the front of body, with the tiptoe on the ground, twist both hands clockwise and withdraw them to the front of body, and withdraw left hand to the inside of right forearm with the palm of left hand downward and that of right hand upward. (Fig 17)

图18

三、懒扎衣
Lazily Tying Coat

1. 屈膝松胯，身法下沉，同时双手左逆右顺缠外掤至胸前。（图18）

Bend knees and loosen crotches, sink bodily movement, meanwhile twist left hand anticlockwise and right hand clockwise and prop them out to the front of chest. (Fig 18)

图19

2. 松左胯，身法下沉，右腿向右横开一步。（图19）

Loosen left crotch, sink bodily movement, and move right leg rightward by a step. (Fig 19)

3. 左胯走前弧，右胯走后弧，身体稍右转重心右移，同时双手左逆右顺缠，左手收至腰间，掌心向上，右手逆缠走上弧外掤至身体右侧，掌心向上，目视右侧。（图20）

Go forward curve with left crotch and backward curve with right crotch, turn body right slightly, and transfer the center of body weight rightward, meanwhile twist left hand anticlockwise and right hand clockwise, and then withdraw left hand to waist, with the palm upward, twist right hand anticlockwise to draw upward curve and prop it out to the right side of body, with the palm upward, and look rightward. (Fig 20)

图20

4. 屈膝松胯，双胯回转，松肩沉肘，气沉丹田。（图21）

Bend knees and loosen crotches, return both crotches, loosen shoulders and sink elbows, and gather *Qi* into *Dantian*. (Fig 21)

图21

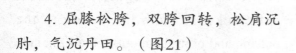

四、上步斜行
Step forward Obliquely

1. 左胯走前弧，右胯走后弧，身体左转，重心左移，同时左腕腹前旋腕顺缠，右手顺缠走上弧里合，掌心向上，双手相合至体前。（图22）

图22

Go forward curve with left crotch and backward curve with right crotch, turn body left, transfer the center of body weight leftward, meanwhile rotate and twist left wrist in front of abdomen, twist right hand to draw upward curve and withdraw inward, with right palm upward, and cross both hands to the front of body. (Fig 22)

图23

2.双胯回转，身体右转，重心右移，同时双手走平圆逆缠由内向外掤至身体右侧，掌心向里。（图23）

Return both crotches, turn body right, transfer the center of body weight rightward, meanwhile draw horizontal circle with both hands, twist them anticlockwise from the inside to the outside and prop them out to the right side of body, with the palms inward. (Fig 23)

图24

3. 左胯走前弧，右胯走后弧，身体左转，重心右移，同时双手左逆右顺缠翻掌外掤，掌心向外。（图24）

Go forward curve with left crotch and backward curve with right crotch, turn body left, and transfer the center of body weight rightward, meanwhile twist left hand anticlockwise and right hand clockwise, overturn both palms and prop them outward, with the palms outward. (Fig 24)

4. 双胯回转，屈膝松胯，身体左转90°，左脚尖外摆，同时左手逆缠立掌外掤至体前，右手顺缠立掌相合至右耳侧。面向东。（图25）

Return both crotches, bend knees and loosen crotches, turn body left by 90°, swing left tiptoe outward, meanwhile twist left hand anticlockwise and prop it out to the front of body with standing palms, twist right hand clockwise and withdraw it to right ear with standing palm. Face eastward. (Fig 25)

图25

5. 屈膝松胯，移重心到左腿，右腿屈膝提起，向右前方45°开一大步，同时左手逆缠下按至体侧，右手顺缠前掤至体前。（图26）

Bend knees and loosen crotches, transfer the center of body weight to left leg, bend right knee to lift and move right forward by 45° by a giant step, meanwhile twist left hand anticlockwise and press it to one side of body, and twist right hand clockwise and prop it forward to the front of body. (Fig 26)

图26

6. 松右胯，提左胯，移重心到右腿，左腿屈膝提起，左腿向左侧前方45°开步，同时右手逆缠下按至体侧，左手顺缠前掤至体前。（图27）

图27

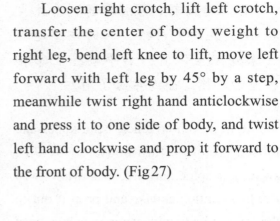

Loosen right crotch, lift left crotch, transfer the center of body weight to right leg, bend left knee to lift, move left forward with left leg by 45° by a step, meanwhile twist right hand anticlockwise and press it to one side of body, and twist left hand clockwise and prop it forward to the front of body. (Fig 27)

图28

7. 左胯走前弧, 右胯走后弧, 身体稍右转, 重心左移, 同时双手左逆右顺缠, 掤至身体前方。（图28）

Go forward curve with left crotch and backward curve with right crotch, turn body right slightly, transfer the center of body weight leftward, meanwhile twist left hand anticlockwise and right hand clockwise and prop them to the front of body. (Fig 28)

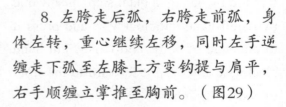

图29

8. 左胯走后弧, 右胯走前弧, 身体左转, 重心继续左移, 同时左手逆缠走下弧至左膝上方变钩提与肩平, 右手顺缠立掌推至胸前。（图29）

Go backward curve with left crotch and forward curve with right crotch, turn body left, transfer the center of body weight leftward continuously, meanwhile twist left hand anticlockwise to draw downward curve to the upside of left knee, change into hook and then lift it to the same level with shoulder, and twist right hand clockwise and push it to the front of chest with standing palm. (Fig 29)

9. 屈膝松胯，左胯走前弧，右胯走后弧，同时，右手逆缠向外划上弧至身体右侧。（图30）

Bend knees and loosen crotches, go forward curve with left crotch and backward curve with right crotch, meanwhile twist right hand anticlockwise and draw upward curve to the right side of body. (Fig 30)

图30

10. 双胯回转，松肩沉肘，气沉丹田，面向东方。（图31）

Return both crotches, loosen shoulders and sink elbows, gather *Qi* into *Dantian*. Face eastward. (Fig 31)

图31

五、上三步
Walking forward Three Steps

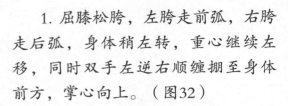

1. 屈膝松胯，左胯走前弧，右胯走后弧，身体稍左转，重心继续左移，同时双手左逆右顺缠掤至身体前方，掌心向上。（图32）

图32

Bend knees and loosen crotches, go forward curve with left crotch and backward curve with right crotch, turn body left slightly, transfer the center of body weight leftward continuously, meanwhile twist left hand anticlockwise and right hand clockwise, and prop them to the front of body, with the palms upward. (Fig 32)

图33

2. 左胯走前弧，右胯走后弧，身体右转，重心右移，同时双手走下弧左顺右逆缠，掤捋至身体右侧下方。（图33）

Go forward curve with left crotch and backward curve with right crotch, turn body right, transfer the center of body weight rightward, meanwhile twist left hand clockwise and right hand anticlockwise to draw downward curve, and prop them to the right downside of body. (Fig 33)

3. 双胯回转，身体左转，重心左移，同时双手左逆右顺缠走上弧，左手立掌掤至体前，右手立掌合至耳侧。（图34）

Return both crotches, turn body left, transfer the center of body weight leftward, meanwhile twist left hand anticlockwise and right hand clockwise to draw upward curve, prop left hand with standing palm to the front of body, and withdraw right hand to ear side with standing palm. (Fig 34)

图34

4. 屈膝松胯，重心转至左腿，右腿屈膝提起，向左前方45°开一大步，同时左手逆缠下按至体侧，右手顺缠前掤至体前。（图35、图36）

Bend knees and loosen crotches, transfer the center of body weight to left leg, bend right knee to lift and move left forward by 45° by a giant step, meanwhile twist left hand anticlockwise and press it to one side of body, and twist right hand clockwise and prop it forward to the front of body. (Fig 35, Fig 36)

图35

5. 以同样的动作要领向前上两步，重心在左腿。

Move forward by two steps with the same gist of movement, and put the center of body weight on left leg.

图36

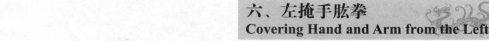

六、左掩手肱拳
Covering Hand and Arm from the Left

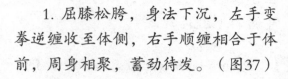

1. 屈膝松胯，身法下沉，左手变拳逆缠收至体侧，右手顺缠相合于体前，周身相聚，蓄劲待发。（图37）

图37

Bend knees and loosen crotches, sink bodily movement, change left hand into fist and twist it anticlockwise and withdraw it to one side of body, twist right hand clockwise and withdraw it to the front of body, and concentrate to exert forces. (Fig 37)

2. 旋腰转膀，左胯走前弧，右胯走后弧，身体迅速右转，左腿扭脚蹬腿，重心快速右移，同时左拳逆缠前冲，右臂逆缠屈肘后击，二者成对拉力，面向正东。（图38）

图38

Rotate waist and shoulders, go forward curve with left crotch and backward curve with right crotch, turn body right rapidly, twist and stretch out left leg, transfer rapidly the center of body weight rightward, meanwhile twist left fist anticlockwise to rush forward and twist right arm anticlockwise and then bend right elbow to attack backward, and both arms supplement each other into a pair of pull. Face eastward. (Fig38)

七、双推手
Push both Hands

1. 屈膝松胯，左拳变掌顺缠，右拳变掌逆缠外掤，右手上合左手于体前。（图39）

Bend knees and loosen crotches, change left fist into palm and twist it clockwise and right fist into palm and twist it anticlockwise to prop outward, and withdraw right hand to left hand in front of body. (Fig 39)

图39

2. 左胯走前弧，右胯走后弧，重心左移，同时双手左逆右顺缠，走下弧掤捋至身体左侧下方。（图40）

Go forward curve with left crotch and backward curve with right crotch, transfer the center of body weight leftward, meanwhile twist left hand anticlockwise and right hand clockwise, draw downward curve to prop them to left downside of body. (Fig 40)

图40

图40附

3. 左胯走后弧，右胯走前弧，身体左转，重心右移，同时双手左逆右顺缠掤捋至身体左侧。（图41）

Go backward curve with left crotch and forward curve with right crotch, turn body left, transfer the center of body weight rightward, meanwhile twist left hand anticlockwise and right hand clockwise and prop them to left side of body. (Fig41)

图41

4. 双胯回旋，身体右转，左腿收至体侧，脚尖点地，同时双手左顺右逆缠，合至胸前，左手立掌，右手伏掌，面向东方。（图42）

Return both crotches, turn body right, withdraw left leg to one side of body with the tiptoe on the ground, meanwhile twist left hand clockwise and right hand anticlockwise, and close them to the front of chest, with left hand into standing palm and right hand into downward palm. Face eastward. (Fig42)

图41附

图42

5. 屈膝松胯。身体下沉，双掌由胸前推出。（图43）

Bend knees and loosen crotches, sink body, and push both palms out before chest. (Fig 43)

图43

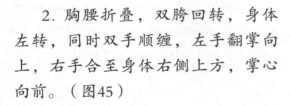

1. 左胯走前弧，右胯走后弧，身体稍右转，同时双手逆缠分开，左掌前推，右拳变掌走下弧至身体右后方。（图44）

Go forward curve with left crotch and backward curve with right crotch, turn body right slightly, meanwhile twist both hands anticlockwise and then separate them, push left palm forward, change right fist into palm and draw downward curve to right backside of body. (Fig 44)

图44

2. 胸腰折叠，双胯回转，身体左转，同时双手顺缠，左手翻掌向上，右手合至身体右侧上方，掌心向前。（图45）

Bend down, return both crotches, turn body left, meanwhile twist both hands clockwise, overturn left palm upward, close right hand to the right upside of body, with the palm forward. (Fig 45)

图45

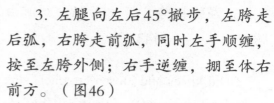

3. 左腿向左后45°撤步，左胯走后弧，右胯走前弧，同时左手顺缠，按至左胯外侧；右手逆缠，掤至体右前方。（图46）

图46

Withdraw left leg left backward by 45°, go backward curve with left crotch and forward curve with right crotch, meanwhile twist left hand clockwise and then press it to the outside of left crotch; twist right hand anticlockwise and then prop it to the right front of body. (Fig 46)

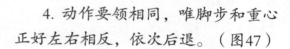

4. 动作要领相同，唯脚步和重心正好左右相反，依次后退。（图47）

The gist of movement is the same as the above, but the footwork and the center of body weight are just reverse; withdraw successively. (Fig 47)

图47

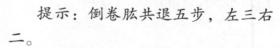

提示：倒卷肱共退五步，左三右二。

Clue: step backward by five steps totally to whirl arms back, with three steps leftward and two steps rightward.

九、闪通背
Flash over the Back

1. 屈膝松胯，身法下沉，左腿屈膝下蹲，右腿仆步下沉，同时左手逆缠外掤至体左侧，右手顺缠下劈至体前下方。（图48）

Bend knees and loosen crotches, sink bodily movement, bend left knee and squat, sink right leg with crouch step, meanwhile twist left hand anticlockwise and prop it to the left side of body and right hand clockwise and hack it to the front downside of body. (Fig 48)

图48

2. 左胯走后弧，右胯走前弧，旋腰转膀，身法上领，重心右移，同时双手左顺右逆缠，左下右上划弧掤至身体两侧。（图49）

Go backward curve with left crotch and forward curve with right crotch, rotate waist and shoulders, uplift bodily movement, transfer the center of body weight rightward, meanwhile twist left hand clockwise and right hand anticlockwise, and draw curve with left hand down and right hand up and prop them to each side of body. (Fig 49)

图49

图50

3. 身法上领，身体右转约45°，同时左腿随体转向前上步，脚跟着地，双手随体转外掤。面向东南。（图50）

Uplift bodily movement, turn body right by about 45°, meanwhile step forward with left leg along with body, with the heel on the ground, and prop out with both hands along with body. Face southeast. (Fig 50)

图51

4. 左胯走前弧，右胯走后弧，身体继续右转45°，重心左移，左脚尖里扣踏实，同时双手左逆右顺缠划弧外掤。面向南。（图51）

Go forward curve with left crotch and backward curve with right crotch, turn body right continuously by 45°, transfer the center of body weight leftward, buckle left tiptoe and step it solidly, meanwhile twist left hand anticlockwise and right hand clockwise, draw curve and prop them outward. Face southward. (Fig 51)

图52

5. 旋腰转膀，身体继续右转90°，右腿后扫回收至左脚里侧成丁字步，同时双手左逆右顺缠相合，左手至体前，右手至身体右侧，双手掌心向上。面向西。（图52）

Rotate waist and shoulders, turn body right continuously by 90°, sweep backward with right leg and withdraw it to the inside of left foot into T-step, meanwhile twist left hand anticlockwise and right hand clockwise and close them, with left hand to the front of body and right leg to the right side of body, with the palms upward. Face westward. (Fig 52)

图53

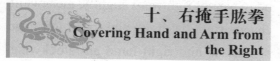

十、右掩手肱拳
Covering Hand and Arm from the Right

屈膝松胯，重心移至右腿，右腿向左前45°开一大步，同时右手变拳与左手相合，含胸塌腰，气归丹田。蓄劲待发。（图53～图56）

Bend knees and loosen crotches, transfer the center of body weight to right leg, move right leg left forward by 45° by a giant step, meanwhile change right hand into fist and close it to left hand, bend down, gather *Qi* into *Dantian*, and store energy to exert force. (Fig 53 - Fig 56)

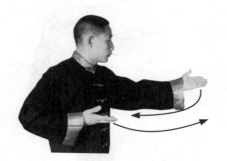

图54

图55

图56

十一、六封四闭
Six Sealing and Four Closing

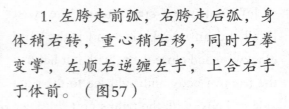

1. 左胯走前弧，右胯走后弧，身体稍右转，重心稍右移，同时右拳变掌，左顺右逆缠左手，上合右手于体前。（图57）

Go forward curve with left crotch and backward curve with right crotch, turn body right slightly, transfer the center of body weight rightward slightly, meanwhile change right fist into palm, twist left hand clockwise and right hand anticlockwise, close left hand up to right hand in front of body. (Fig 57)

图57

2. 身体左转，重心继续右移，左脚尖外摆，同时双手左逆右顺缠随体转外掤。（图58）

Turn body left, transfer the center of body weight rightward continuously, swing left tiptoe outward, meanwhile twist left hand anticlockwise and right hand clockwise, and prop them outward along with body. (Fig 58)

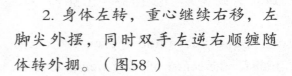

图58

3. 左脚踏实，屈膝松胯，重心移至左腿，双手外掤。（图59）

Step left foot solidly, bend knees and loosen crotches, transfer the center of body weight to left leg and prop outward with both hands. (Fig 59)

图59

4. 松左胯，身体继续左转，同时右腿屈膝提起。（图60）

Loosen left crotch, turn body left continuously, and meanwhile bend right knee to lift. (Fig 60)

图60

5. 右腿向右侧45°开一步，同时双手稍向左掤。（图61）

Move right leg rightward by 45° by a step, and meanwhile prop leftward slightly with both hands. (Fig 61)

图61

6. 屈膝松胯，左胯走后弧，右胯走前弧，重心右移，同时双手左顺右逆缠上掤至体侧。（图62）

图62

Bend knees and loosen crotches, go backward curve with left crotch and forward curve with right crotch, transfer the center of body weight rightward, meanwhile twist left hand clockwise and right hand anticlockwise and prop them up to one side of body. (Fig 62)

7. 屈膝松胯，左胯走前弧，右胯走后弧，身体稍右转，同时双手合至体前，左手立掌，右手掌心向下。（图63）

图63

Bend knees and loosen crotches, go forward curve with left crotch and backward curve with right crotch, turn body right slightly, meanwhile close both hands to the front of body, with left standing palm and right palm downward. (Fig 63)

图64

8. 重心移至右腿，左腿收至体侧，脚尖点地。（图64）

Transfer the center of body weight to right leg, and withdraw left leg on one side of body, with the tiptoe on the ground. (Fig 64)

9. 双掌从胸前推出，掌心斜向外，松肩沉肘，气沉丹田。（图65）

Push both palms out before chest, with palms obliquely outward, loosen shoulders and sink elbows and gather *Qi* into *Dantian*. (Fig 65)

图65

 十二、运手
Moving Hands

1. 屈膝松胯，身体左转，同时双手左逆右顺缠，左下右上划弧掤挒至体左前方。（图66）

Bend knees and loosen crotches, turn body left, meanwhile twist left hand anticlockwise and right hand clockwise, draw curve with left hand down and right hand up, and prop them to the left front of body. (Fig 66)

图66

2. 双手左顺右逆缠，左下右上划弧，掤挒至体右前方，同时左脚配合双手向左侧横开一步。（图67）

Twist left hand clockwise and right hand anticlockwise, draw curve with left hand down and right hand up, prop them to the right front of body, and meanwhile move left foot leftward by a step along with the movement of both hands. (Fig 67)

图67

图68

3. 左胯走前弧，右胯走后弧，重心移至左腿，右腿收至左腿内侧，同时双手左逆右顺缠，左上右下划弧掤捋至体左前方。（图68）

Go forward curve with left crotch and backward curve with right crotch, transfer the center of body weight to left leg, withdraw right leg to the inside of left leg, meanwhile twist left hand anticlockwise and right hand clockwise, and draw curve with left hand up and right hand down, and prop them to the left front of body. (Fig 68)

图69

4. 双胯回转，屈膝松胯，重心移至右腿，同时双手左顺右逆缠，左下右上划弧掤捋至体右前方，同时左脚配合双手向左侧横开一步。（图69）

Return both crotches, bend knees and loosen crotches, transfer the center of body weight to right leg, meanwhile twist left hand clockwise and right hand anticlockwise, draw curve with left hand down and right hand up, and prop them to the right front of body, and meanwhile move left foot leftward by a step along with the movement of both hands. (Fig 69)

5. 动作要领同前边的步法要领，共向左移动四步。（图70）

The gist of movement is the same as that of the above footwork, and move leftward by four steps. (Fig 70)

图70

十三、高探马
Pat the Horse High

1. 左胯走后弧，右胯走前弧，身体左转，重心左移，右脚尖里扣，同时双手左逆右顺缠，左上右下划弧外掤。（图71）

Go backward curve with left crotch and forward curve with right crotch, turn body left, transfer the center of body weight leftward, buckle right tiptoe inward, meanwhile twist left hand anticlockwise and right hand clockwise, and draw curve with left hand up and right hand down, and prop them outward. (Fig 71)

图71

2. 身体继续左转，重心移至右腿，左脚尖外摆，同时双手左顺右逆缠，左下右上划弧外掤。面向东。（图72）

Turn body left continuously, transfer the center of body weight to right leg, swing left tiptoe outward, twist left hand clockwise and right hand anticlockwise,

图72

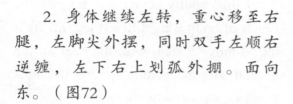

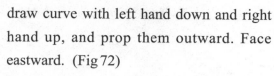

draw curve with left hand down and right hand up, and prop them outward. Face eastward. (Fig 72)

图73

3. 屈膝松胯，胸腰折叠，身体继续左转90°，重心左移，左脚踏实，同时双手顺缠相合；右手屈肘合至身体右侧上方，左手合于右肘下侧，掌心向上。面向北。（图73）

Bend knees and loosen crotches, bend down, turn body left continuously by 90°, transfer the center of body weight leftward, step left foot solidly, meanwhile twist both hands clockwise and close them; bend right elbow to the right upside of body, close left hand to the downside of right elbow, with palms upward. Face northward. (Fig 73)

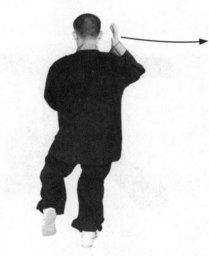

图74

4. 身法上领，重心移至左腿，右腿上提开步，脚跟着地，同时双手继续顺缠里合。（图74、图74附）

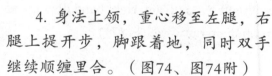

Uplift bodily movement, transfer the center of body weight to left leg, lift right leg to move a step, with the heel on the ground, and meanwhile twist both hands clockwise continuously to close inward. (Fig 74, Fig 74App)

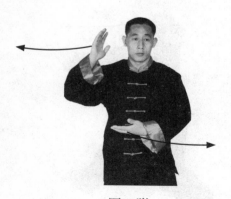

图74附

5. 屈膝松胯，胸腰折叠，重心移至右腿，左脚尖点地，同时左手逆缠走下弧收至左腰间，右手逆缠向右侧推出。面向北。（图75、图75附）

Bend knees and loosen crotches, bend down, transfer the center of body weight to right leg, with left tiptoe on the ground, meanwhile twist left hand anticlockwise to draw downward curve to left waist, twist right hand anticlockwise and push it out rightward. Face northward. (Fig 75, Fig 75App)

图75

十四、右蹬一跟
Kick with the Right Heel

1. 松右胯，身体右转，同时双手顺缠，左手上合，右手外掤。（图76、图76附）

Loosen right crotch, turn body right, and meanwhile twist both hands clockwise, with left hand closing upward and right hand propping outward. (Fig 76, Fig 76App)

图75附

图76附

图76

2. 身体左转，双手逆缠左下右上分至体两侧，掌心斜向下，同时左腿屈膝上提。（图77）

Turn body left, twist both hands anticlockwise with left hand down and right hand up to separate them to each side of body, with palms obliquely downward, and meanwhile bend left knee to lift. (Fig 77)

图77

3. 左腿在右腿前交叉盖步，脚跟着地，同时双手顺缠交叉里合。左掌心向下，右掌心向上。（图78）

Move left leg to the front of right leg with cross step, with left heel on the ground, meanwhile twist both hands clockwise and cross to close inward, with left palm downward and right palm upward. (Fig 78)

图78

4. 移重心到左腿，同时双手逆缠外撑至体前。（图79、图79附）

Transfer the center of body weight to left leg, and meanwhile twist both hands anticlockwise to prop them outward to the front of body. (Fig 79, Fig 79App)

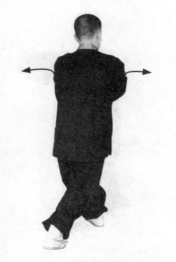

图79

5. 松左胯，身法上领，右腿屈膝提起。（图80、图80附）

Loosen left crotch, uplift bodily movement, and bend right knee to lift. (Fig 80, Fig 80App)

图79附

图80

图80附

6. 右腿向右侧蹬出，同时双手逆缠向两侧发力推出，三力同时发出。（图81）

Kick right leg rightward, meanwhile twist both hands anticlockwise to exert force to each side, and exert these three forces simultaneously. (Fig 81)

图81

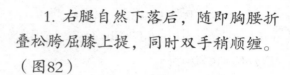

十五、左蹬一跟
Kick with the Left Heel

图82

1. 右腿自然下落后，随即胸腰折叠松胯屈膝上提，同时双手稍顺缠。（图82）

Fall right leg down naturally, bend down, loosen crotches to lift, and meanwhile twist both hands clockwise slightly. (Fig 82)

图83

2. 松左胯，身体右转90°，右腿交叉盖步于体前，脚跟着地，脚尖外摆，同时双手顺缠交叉相合于体前，掌心向上。面向东。（图83）

Loosen left crotch, turn body right by 90°, move right leg by cross step in front of body, with the heel on the ground, swing the tiptoe outward, meanwhile twist both hands clockwise and cross to close them in front of body, with palms upward. Face eastward. (Fig 83)

图84

3. 重心移至右腿，身体继续右转90°，同时双手逆缠外撑至体前。面向南。（图84）

Transfer the center of body weight to right leg, turn body right continuously by 90°, meanwhile twist both hands anticlockwise and support them outward to the front of body. Face southward. (Fig 84)

4. 松右胯，身法上领，左腿屈膝提起。（图85）

Loosen right crotch, uplift bodily movement, and bend left knee to lift. (Fig 85)

图85

5. 左脚向左侧蹬出，同时双手逆缠向两侧发力推出。三力要同时发出。面向南。（图86）

Kick left leg leftward, meanwhile twist both hands anticlockwise to exert force to each side, and exert these three forces simultaneously. Face southward. (Fig 86)

图86

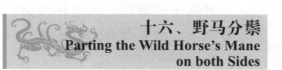
1. 松右胯，身体稍右转，左腿屈膝回收，落于体左侧，同时双手顺缠里合，左上右下划弧至身体两侧。（图87）

Loosen right crotch, turn body right slightly, bend left knee to withdraw and fall left foot down to the left side of body, meanwhile twist both hands clockwise and close inward, and draw curve with left hand up and right hand down to each side of body. (Fig 87)

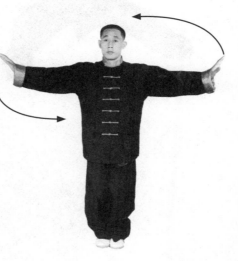

图87

2. 屈膝松胯，左胯走前弧，右胯走后弧，重心移至左腿，左腿屈膝下沉，右腿向右后侧45°开一大步，同时双手顺缠左下右上划弧，相合至体前。（图88）

图88

Bend knees and loosen crotches, go forward curve with left crotch and backward curve with right crotch, transfer the center of body weight to left leg, bend left knee to sink, move right leg right backward by 45° by a giant step, meanwhile twist both hands clockwise, draw curve with left hand down and right hand up and close them to the front of body. (Fig 88)

3. 双胯回转，身体右转，重心右移，同时双手逆缠外分至身体两侧，左掌心向下，右掌心向上。（图89）

图89

Return both crotches, turn body right, transfer the center of body weight rightward, and meanwhile twist both hands anticlockwise and separate them outward to each side of body, with left palm downward and right palm upward. (Fig 89)

4. 双胯回转，身体继续右转约45°，重心移至左腿，右脚尖外摆，同时双手顺缠，翻掌合至体前，左下右上，掌心相对。（图90）

Return both crotches, turn body right continuously by about 45°, transfer the center of body weight to left leg, swing right tiptoe outward, meanwhile twist both hands clockwise turn palms over in front of body, with left palm down and right palm up, and with both palms face to face. (Fig 90)

图90

5. 身体继续右转约45°，重心移至右腿，左腿屈膝提起。面向北。（图91）

Turn body right continuously by about 45°, transfer the center of body weight to right leg, bend left knee to lift. Face northward. (Fig 91)

图91

6. 屈膝松胯，右腿屈膝下沉，左腿向左后侧45°开一大步，同时双手随体转相合至体前。（图92）

Bend knees and loosen crotches, bend right knee to sink, move left leg left backward by 45° by a giant step, and meanwhile close both hands to the front of body along with turning body. (Fig 92)

图92

7．双胯回转，身体左转，重心左移，同时双手逆缠外分至身体两侧，左掌心向上，右掌心向下。面向北。（图93）

Return both crotches, turn body left, transfer the center of body weight leftward, meanwhile twist both hands anticlockwise and separate them outward to each side of body, with left palm upward and right palm downward. Face northward. (Fig 93)

图93

十七、玉女穿梭
The Beauty Works at the Shuttle

1．身体稍左一转，右手顺缠上合左手于身体左侧。（图94）

Turn body left slightly, twist right hand clockwise and close upward to left hand on left side of body. (Fig 94)

图94

2．左胯走前弧，右胯走后弧，身体稍右转，重心右移，同时双手左顺右逆缠下将至身体右侧下方。（图95）

Go forward curve with left crotch and backward curve with right crotch, turn body right slightly, transfer the center of body weight rightward, meanwhile twist left hand clockwise and right hand

图95

anticlockwise and rub them downward to right downside of body. (Fig 95)

3. 双胯回转，身体左转45°，重心左移，同时双手左逆右顺缠走上弧外掤至体侧。左手掌心向前，右手屈肘里合至右肩外侧。面向北。（图96）

Return both crotches, turn body left by 45°, transfer the center of body weight leftward, meanwhile twist left hand anticlockwise and right hand clockwise to draw upward curve and prop them out to one side of body, with left palm forward, bend right elbow and close it inward to the outside of right shoulder. Face northward. (Fig 96)

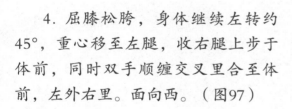

图96

4. 屈膝松胯，身体继续左转约45°，重心移至左腿，收右腿上步于体前，同时双手顺缠交叉里合至体前，左外右里。面向西。（图97）

Bend knees and loosen crotches, turn body left continuously by about 45°, transfer the center of body weight to left leg, withdraw right leg and step it to the front of body, meanwhile twist both hands clockwise and cross and close them inward in front of body, with left hand outward and right hand inward. Face westward. (Fig 97)

图97

5. 胸腰折叠，左手围绕右手由里向外，先顺后逆，旋腕缠绕一周，置于右小臂内侧。（图98）

Bend down, twist left hand around right hand from inside to outside clockwise and then anticlockwise, rotate the wrist by a circle to the inside of right forearm. (Fig 98)

图98

6. 双手胸前逆缠，以缠丝劲领起全身，右腿屈膝上提，右脚蹬地跃起。（图99）

Twist both hands in front of chest, uplift the whole body with twisting forces, bend right knee to lift, and stamp against the ground with right foot to leap. (Fig 99)

图99

7. 双脚左先右后震脚落地，同时双手顺缠下按。（图100）

Stamp to fall down to the ground with left foot and then right foot successively, meanwhile twist both hands clockwise and press down. (Fig 100)

图100

8. 屈膝松胯，胸腰折叠，右腿屈膝上提，同时双手逆缠里合至胸前。（图101）

Bend knees and loosen crotches, bend down, bend right knee to lift, meanwhile twist both hands anticlockwise and close them inward to the front of chest. (Fig 101)

图101

9. 身体左转，右脚向右侧蹬出，同时左臂屈肘后击，右掌快速前推，三力同时发出。（图102）

Turn body left, kick out rightward with right foot, meanwhile bend left elbow to attack backward, push right palm forward rapidly, and exert these three forces simultaneously. (Fig 102)

图102

10. 重心前移，右脚前迈落地，迅速移重心到右腿并蹬地向前跃起，身体右转约180°，带动左腿向前跃进一大步，同时左掌向前发力推出，右臂屈肘后击，左脚落地后，身体继续向右转体180°，右脚向右横开一步，同时双手左逆右顺缠左上右下划弧相合于胸前。（图103、图104）

Transfer the center of body weight forward, stride right foot and fall down, transfer the center of body weight to right

图103

leg and stamp against to leap forward, turn body right by about 180° to bring left leg to leap forward by a giant step, meanwhile exert forces forward with left palm and push it out, bend right elbow to attack backward, stamp left foot to fall down to the ground, then turn body right continuously by 180°, move right foot rightward by a step, meanwhile twist left hand anticlockwise and right hand clockwise, and draw curves with left hand up and right hand down and close them in front of chest. (Fig 103, Fig 104)

图104

11. 屈膝松胯，重心右移，同时双手逆缠左下右上划弧分至身体两侧。面向南。（图105）

Bend knees and loosen crotches, transfer the center of body weight rightward, meanwhile twist both hands anticlockwise with left hand down and right hand up, draw curve to separate them to each side of body. Face southward. (Fig 105)

图105

十八、金刚捣碓
Buddha's Warrior Pounding Mortar

1. 左胯走前弧，右胯走后弧，重心移至左腿，右腿划后弧收至身前，前脚掌点地，双手顺缠合至体前，左手掌心向下合于右小臂内侧，右手掌心向上。（图106）

Go forward curve with left crotch and backward curve with right crotch, transfer the center of body weight to left leg, draw backward curve with right leg and withdraw to the front of body, with anterior sole on the ground, twist both hands and close them to the front of body, close left hand downward to the inside of right forearm, with left palm downward and right palm upward. (Fig 106)

图106

2. 屈膝松胯，胸腰折叠，身法下沉，左手逆缠外翻，右手变拳随体下沉至腹前。（图107）

Bend knees and loosen crotches, bend down, sink bodily movement, twist left hand and turn it outward, change right hand into fist and sink it to the front of abdomen along with body. (Fig 107)

图107

3. 右拳顺缠上冲，领右腿屈膝上提。（图108）

Twist right fist clockwise and rush upward, uplift right leg and bend right knee to lift. (Fig 108)

图108

4. 右脚震脚落地，同时右拳快速落入左掌心，重心调至两腿之间，气沉丹田。（图109）

Stamp right foot and fall it down to the ground, meanwhile fall right fist rapidly into left palm, adjust the center of body weight between both legs, and gather *Qi* into *Dantian*. (Fig 109)

图109

十九、收势
Closing Form

1. 屈膝松胯，身法下沉，双手逆缠外分至身体两侧，掌心相对。（图110）

Bend knees and loosen crotches, sink bodily movement, twist anticlockwise with both hands anticlockwise and separate them to each side of body, with both palms face to face. (Fig 110)

图110

2. 双手顺缠上合，平屈肘于胸前，掌心向下。（图111）

Twist both hands clockwise and close them upward, bend elbows horizontally in front of chest, with palms downward. (Fig 111)

图111

3. 屈膝松胯，身法下沉，双手逆缠下按分至身体两侧。（图112）

Bend knees and loosen crotches, sink bodily movement, twist both hands anticlockwise and press them separately to each side of body. (Fig 112)

图112

4. 身法上领，左腿收于右腿内侧，随即还原成立正姿势，气归丹田。（图113）

Uplift bodily movement, withdraw left leg to the inside of right leg, then return to the form of standing straightly, and gather *Qi* into *Dantian*. (Fig 113)

图113

陈家沟太极拳学校简介
A Brief Introduction to Chenjiagou Taijiquan School

陈家沟太极拳学校1982年建校，是国内建校最早的一所太极拳专业学校，学员来自全国乃至世界各地。现任校长为陈氏第十九世太极拳掌门人陈小旺，执行校长为国际太极拳大师陈小星（兴）。

现开设有：普修班、进修班、教练员班、健身班、推手班、太极散手班、假期班、假日班等。

This school was set up in 1982 and is the earliest professional school of Taijiquan in China. Learners come from home and abroad. The current president is the 19th generation Chen Family Taijiquan authority, Chen Xiaowang, and the executive president is Chen Xiaoxing, an international Taijiquan master.

The classes available include: Class for general studies, Class for advanced studies, Class for coaches, Class for body-building, Class for push-hands, Class for Taiji free combat, Class for vacations, Class for holidays.

通信地址： 河南省温县陈家沟太极拳学校

Address: Chenjiagou Taijiquan School, Wen County, Henan Province

邮编： 454865

P.C: 454865

电话/传真： +86-391-6416456

Tel/Fax: +86-391-6416456

网址： www.tjqxx.com

Website: www.tjqxx.com

电子邮箱： taijiquanxuexiao@yahoo.com.cn

E-mail: taijiquanxuexiao@yahoo.com.cn